A MAP YOU CANNOT REFOLD

A MAP YOU CANNOT REFOLD

DANIELLE SHONTAE SMITH

Danielle Shontae Smith

A Map You Cannot Refold
ISBN (print): 979-8-9853962-0-1
ISBN (eBook): 979-8-9853962-1-8

for the survivors who have lived the content

Contents

Dedication   v

19 Minutes   1

Content Note   2

Why I Haven't Watched My TEDx Talk   3

Hear Me More   9

I
TALK TO ME LIKE A BLACK GIRL!

Revision   16

Bones   20

Who Were We?   31

In the Beginning   32

A Girl Who Loves Stories   34

Scenes   36

A Space Between   43

Welcome Home   46

A Long Time Comin'   49

II

SMART FOR A (BLACK) GIRL

Admission   54

Gestures   57

The Keychain   60

May I have your attention, please?   62

Lesson. Plan.   64

Like   65

You're SO articulate!   67

So, tell me about yourself.   68

Transcript   71

Qualified   78

Student Life   81

School Girl   86

Critics   88

III
WILL YOU TAKE THIS, WOMAN?

Content Note   96

Call And Response   97

Song for My Beloved I: Loving   98

Ablation   101

The Door Frame   103

The Writing of Fiction   104

Slam   107

The Rules   110

Black, Radical Feminist   111

A Woman's Study   112

References   115

On Consoling Men Who Cry   118

7 things   123

Rough Draft   125

Processing...   126

Aftermath   127

Request   129

Catalogue   133

Cause & Effect   136

Asking for It   138

Stop   139

Frequently Asked Questions (FAQs)   140

Stories   141

IV
A WOMAN'S WORK

Disembodied   144

Hunger   145

Wheezy   147

Body Image   154

Recovery   161

Hands   164

An Education   165

For Your Information 167

Critical Personal Narrative 169

Yes, You Can 178

The Grammar of Me 180

On the Surface 182

Hands (Reprise) 183

dear lucille 184

Note to Self 187

Claiming Space (Reprise) 191

Epilogue 197
Resources 199
Permissions 201
With Gratitude 203
About the Author 204

19 Minutes

On June 1, 2013, I stood on a stage with a microphone taped to my face and engaged in the most vulnerable act of my life to date.

As I spoke, I hoped my message would reach someone who needed to hear it. Also, as I spoke, I hoped the video carrying my message would get lost on the internet, and no one would ever watch it. While I used to judge myself rather harshly for this seeming contradiction, I have recently begun to practice the art of sitting with complexity.

To provide context for this book, I considered including the script of my talk and other relevant materials, such as The Email. But a persistent voice kept saying to me, "Just let them watch." If you read my script, you would know the words I used, but reading my words on the page would not adequately reflect my experience on that stage.

Those 19 minutes hold some stories and voices that I don't repeat here but are intricately connected to what you will read. I am asking for 19 more minutes of your time so you can hear them.

By watching, you will not only better understand the book you're about to read, but you will also help me live more bravely. Here's how:

1. Visit ted.com/tedx/events/7086
2. Look for "Event videos."
3. Watch "Claiming Space."
4. Come back.

See you in 19 minutes.

Content Note

Content warnings (CW) inform the audience that subject matter may provoke a strong psychological or physiological response. The purpose of a content warning is to prepare the audience so they can make informed decisions regarding if, when, and/or how they wish to engage with the content.

Some chapters in this book reference disordered eating and body image, mental health conditions, emotional abuse, and sexualized violence; therefore, I include content warnings at the beginning of chapters that contain sensitive topics, as some readers may find the content upsetting. I strive to include only as much detail as necessary to share the story without providing graphic descriptions that could be retraumatizing or distressing (to me or my readers). To this end, I write about some topics in general terms or with brief references only.

As an imperfect human being, I may not have recognized or identified every instance that could potentially cause an adverse psychological or physiological response. Our lived experiences are individual and varied, and, likewise, so are our emotional responses and boundaries. I invite you to engage with this book in a way that honors yours.

Thank you for reading,

Danielle

Why I Haven't Watched My TEDx Talk

Prologue

CW: Brief mention of body image disturbance and disordered eating behavior

Because I will simply look at myself and hate everything I see.

Because the year was 2013, and I still had, perhaps, 40 unwanted pounds remaining on my body. The culprit? Emotional eating. *Its* cause? Covertly plotting to leave my toxic, cohabiting relationship was much more complicated and had taken a lot longer than expected. I admitted in the talk that one of the first thoughts I had after learning I was selected to speak was *How much weight can I lose by June 1st?* The sad truth is I was disappointed that I'd had seven weeks to lose weight— to engage in the unhealthy calorie restriction and over-exercising with which I was much too familiar—but, in those seven weeks, I had not given into those impulses, and I didn't lose any weight.

Because I hated the outfit I picked out. Why did I wear that?! The night before, I spent hours shopping, trying to recreate the look I'd seen other female speakers wear: nice jeans, a feminine top, and some flats. I couldn't find any jeans I liked, so I chose slacks. I convinced myself I needed to buy a sweater because I hated how my arms looked; they weren't the same toned arms I once had. My slacks were wrinkled from sitting. The flats I bought rubbed the back of my foot raw. I felt frumpy and was uncomfortable the entire time.

Because I know I will hate the way I pronounced a word, or I will notice the absence of yet another thing I wish I had said. When I originally wrote my talk, I wanted to close with a quote by Molly Crabapple, an artist and writer I had recently discovered. Toward the end of her gorgeous article "Diego, Frida, and Me," Crabapple has a message for women and artists: "Explore the radical possibilities of facing outwards. Take up space. Be big." I loved those words. I thought they stated so well what I wanted to say; however, I don't recall why I didn't include them. I wish I had. Perhaps I feared I wasn't an animated or vibrant enough speaker to end in the way I wanted. Perhaps I felt that I didn't deserve to speak those words.

Because I could imagine someone stumbling across my video one day and saying, "Oh, geez. This isn't what a TED Talk should be. They'll let just *anybody* do a TED Talk these days."

* * *

Hosted by Western Washington University's Student Outreach Services (SOS), the inaugural TEDxWWU was curated specifically for the department's student population: first in their families to attend college, historically underrepresented and underserved, or with high financial need. Students with similar backgrounds to my own.

Led by event organizer Marli Williams, the planning team selected the theme "Renovations: Building Our Future" to apply to this target audience directly. They wanted speakers to deliver messages that would be meaningful for their students to hear. When coming to college, these students often struggle to transition between their home communities and university because the two sites are often in conflict. In the academy, educators often tell students (indirectly or directly) that their previous ways of knowing and being are inadequate. Educators often view students through a lens of deficit, not strength. Our educational institutions ask a lot of our students: tuition and fees, years of study, patience as they navigate bureaucratic red tape, school pride.

What educators don't ask themselves nearly enough: From what rich foundations do our students draw? What aspects of their identities do students feel they must leave at home to be accepted on campus? What parts of themselves must they leave behind on campus to still be accepted at home?

Caught between these two worlds, many students begin to feel that they exist in a space between—trying so hard to fit in everywhere that they eventually belong nowhere.

Well, I thought, what if I told these students about the deep shame I experienced after finally accepting that I had devalued the lessons my family had taught me because they hadn't gone to college and weren't "properly credentialed"? What if I told them about my internalized oppression that contributed to a lifetime of self-erasure?

Yes, I would tell them that.

I thought about impostor syndrome, about feeling inadequate, that I didn't matter. What if I shared two stories about people who made me feel that I mattered? Two deceptively ordinary interactions with people who have subsequently impacted me so much that my life could never have possibly been the same after meeting them. If nothing else, I would have the opportunity to tell an audience of 150 and an unknowable number of future viewers about George: a man I will never have the chance to know better, but a man who has taught me, perhaps, the most valuable lesson of all my years.

Yes, I would share that.

What if I shared how deeply nervous I was to speak publicly, especially about such vulnerable topics? Someone I deeply respect once said to me, "You know, every time you get up to speak, you always say that you're no good at it. When you say that, you give away your power. What you *want* to do is go up there and not let them know you're nervous."

No. That's what *you* want to do.

As I was living my own story, she created a different story. First, she hadn't heard what I had been saying. I never once said I wasn't a good speaker; she had misunderstood, thinking I didn't believe in myself. I said that I *didn't like* speaking in public, and I only reluctantly spoke at events because my role on campus required as much, which is true. Second, I often begin by sharing how nervous I am because I believe there's already enough posturing. As a result, so many spectators look at the speaker on stage, believing that the speaker must possess some magic that they themselves do not. They think *I could never do that!* Rather than contribute to more posturing and feign confidence, I wanted to communicate that you can be nervous or afraid or anxious and still speak. So. What if I showed I was nervous, but I stood up there and spoke anyway?

Yes, I would show them that.

Speaking at TEDx, the stakes were high. Like millions, I *love* TED Talks. I watch them for my own edification, and I've used them while teaching classes. To prepare for my own talk, I sought inspiration by rewatching my favorite TED Talks, adding to their existing tens of millions of views. I would have loved to deliver a talk like any of those. As I watched the speakers deliver their talks in a manner that seemed effortless, what began as an exercise in inspiration led to one of comparison.

In the weeks leading up to the talk, I could barely sleep due to anxiety. In late May, deep in my anxiety storm, I met with Marli and asked to use a script and podium. She replied, "That's not what a TED Talk *is*. You just need to get up there and own it!" I replied that she, an outgoing extrovert, could perhaps get up on stage and "own it." I, a shy introvert, don't *own* things. Regardless, she told me she believed in me and that I was capable. I left our talk trying to borrow her confidence in me.

After another sleepless night, the week of the event, I left a panicked voicemail pleading with Marli again to let me use a script and a podium. In the morning, she agreed and said she'd make it happen. I was a bit relieved, but only just. Though I hadn't spoken to God in a while, I sent a prayer of thanks up to Heaven.

The day before TEDxWWU, I stood on stage in front of a microphone, facing the empty chairs where the audience would soon be. At rehearsal, I could barely get through my talk without crying. I bumbled through my script, shaking and in tears. On stage, looking past the bright spotlights to the intimidating 1,040 seat theater, I stopped every few minutes as I got emotionally overwhelmed. Each time I had to stop to collect myself, I cried, "I'm sorry, Marli!" into the microphone. I thought I was letting her down because I wasn't the confident speaker she had encouraged me to be. I looked out at the rows of seats and saw our speaking coach observing, along with Swil Kanim and other speakers who were waiting to rehearse. I was so embarrassed. Twenty or so minutes later—my body practically vibrating—I stepped off stage. After I descended the stairs, Swil stood up and gave me a body-encompassing hug. And as he held me, we both sobbed. I had just met him. I have not seen Swil since TEDx, but that moment is one I will never forget.

* * *

"Why don't you like yourself?" my mother asked me at the post-event reception. I was standing in a room amongst 150 people, holding a six-inch, square paper plate dotted with cubes of Gouda cheese and quartered strawberries. How very fitting of my mother to ask such a question at this moment. I had no easy answer. Who *does* have an easy answer in response to that question? If you *do* have a response to such a question ready on your lips, I don't know if I should hug you or be impressed that you can articulate your self-hatred so succinctly. I think I want to hug you.

When I wrote my talk, I thought maybe there was a person in the audience or someone who would later watch my talk on the internet who had experienced some of the same vulnerability, shame, or insecurity as I have. In my talk, I said, "You don't know who your presence might reach." I meant that. But, for my mental health, I don't read comments on the internet, so I won't know what strangers will think about my talk.

What *do* I know? I had multiple people approach me afterward, telling me how much they appreciated my talk and how deeply my words and stories impacted them.

At the reception, there was a wall on which attendees could write lessons learned from the talks. An SOS student employee I knew well came to me, grabbed my elbow, and said, "Come here. I want to show you something." She pulled me to the wall and showed me where a student had scribbled, "*I want to <u>claim</u> my education and not just receive one.*" I stood there with her and cried.

No, I haven't watched my TEDx Talk, and I don't tell people I've done one. I'll probably never list "TEDx speaker" in my LinkedIn headline or email signature.

But if someone stumbles upon the talk one day and something I said connects with them, then I have done what I set out to do.

"Why I Haven't Watched My TEDx Talk" was originally posted to my website on 07/27/2018 and has since been lightly revised.

Hear Me More

An Introduction

"When I get older, I'm gonna wear shoes that make noise so people know I'm coming." Heels. Tap shoes. Whatever.

When I was a young girl, I would say these words to my mother. I wanted people to hear my feet land when I walked so they knew I was on my way. They needed to get ready. Ready for what? I'm not sure. But whatever it was, I needed them to prepare.

I also loved words, so I used a lot of them.

"Miss Smith, you have diarrhea of the mouth!" My sixth-grade art teacher clearly loved words too, because she asserted herself in such a vibrant way. When I wouldn't stop talking or passing notes even after her warnings, she would throw her hands up in exasperation and walk away saying, "Cheese and crackers!" What a woman.

How does a child who wanted everyone around her to hear the landing of her feet come to be a woman who utters the words, "Why do I feel guilty for existing?"?

How am I so quiet and timid all of a sudden? When did I become so un-recognizable to myself? What was the catalyzing moment? I sat and thought but nothing came.

If it did happen abruptly, though, shouldn't I have felt something?

Instead, am I in my record scratch moment? Like that trope in movies or TV shows when the scene catches a character in a freeze frame, then the voice-over chimes in to say, "How did I get here? Let's review..." and then tells their story in flashback?

Let's review.

What if it wasn't so *all at once*? Might it have been an accumulation of experiences just subtle enough to escape my notice?

There must be evidence somewhere.

I started reading through notebooks and journals. Those led me to thumb drives, external hard drives, loose scraps of paper, emails, text messages, medical records and healthcare portal messages, the cloud, sticky notes, yearbooks, transcripts, standardized test scores.

Years of the stories of me.

I found plenty of lighthearted notes to myself holding lessons that— at the time of writing—I am still learning.

M, 30 Jan 2017

danielle! Remember on this day: Coffee does not like you, though you may like it. The feeling is not mutual. Stop hurting yourself. The End. (actually, this isn't the end; you made the conscious decision to order coffee yesterday, asked J. to make you a shot of espresso this morning, AND THEN you added coffee to your cup at the colloquium this morn- ing. STOP BEING THE SOURCE OF YOUR OWN PAIN!)

Then I found a series of entries that were *slightly* less lighthearted. They gave me pause.

UNDATED ENTRY
I'm not quite sure what I thought life would be like at age 32. All I know is: it's not this. I guess the lesson (and I get it) is that we never

I didn't finish the thought. What did I "get"? What was the lesson? What had I figured out at age 32?

UNDATED ENTRY
I want to be happy now. Not in one year. I have the audaciousness to think that I deserve happiness.

Who told you that you deserved anything?

UNDATED ENTRY
What I recognize about myself is that I live only to hide.

I don't remember writing any of those entries. What state of mind or heart must I have been in that I have no memory of writing these words?

> *9 May 2019*
> *I am so fucking angry that I have lived my life as a people-pleaser. I am angry that I have rarely given myself permission to actually admit and express just how angry I am (weird form of meta-anger?).*
> *I feel as though I am going to burst wide open. I'm on the brink of some serious rage outbursts if I don't address this soon.*
> *How many times... HOW MANY TIMES have I said, "It's okay" or "it's fine" and didn't mean it? Too many. Because it's not fucking fine.*
> *Why is it so important to me that people like me and think I'm nice?*
> *Why did I say, "I shouldn't have driven him home. I shouldn't have gone inside his apartment."?*
> *Why did those guys get away with it? Why did they get upset with me because I dared speak up and say what they were doing wasn't okay? And why did I feel slightly guilty?*

This I do remember writing. Hard to forget.

I was reading an anthology of essays by people across the gender spectrum, but primarily women, about their experiences of violence, sexual assault, and harassment. How their experiences were often ig-nored, denied, questioned, or justified—even, sometimes, by themselves.

I grabbed my journal, sat on the patio of my apartment, and started to write.

The Danielle who wrote those words was not fine, and she was also right. You can only accept so much before your foundation begins to crack.

For years, I found ways to explain how I felt...but never to anyone directly. In a poem I wrote about the day I graduated from college ("I Can't Decide Between Saint and Sinner, So I Wrap Both in One Frilly Dress"), I recall the moment when my family was taking pictures. I described myself as a "poseable doll in rapid shutter shots." They told me where to stand, so I stood. They told me what to wear, so I wore.

Poseable doll.

"I feel fragmented. I don't know the word for it. I just know that I'm a different person in so many groups and different with my family than with my friends. I don't know..."

"Inauthentic?" my therapist offers.

Yes, inauthentic. That was the word. But "fragmented" is an apt description. I feel that I had been just waiting for directions: "Who do you need me to be right now?"

An accumulation of experiences just subtle enough to escape my notice? Not subtle. I *knew.* I noticed everything, but I swallowed all emotions that arose when I began to feel the impact of noticing everything while confronting nothing. And I believed there was no consequence to my doing so.

* * *

In preparation for my TEDx Talk, the advice was, "Have one central message. Give the talk of your life." Was there a central message of my talk? Perhaps. I spoke about the importance of examining our educations beyond *formal* education.

Often, we learn that there is one *true* education: the one we receive from formal schooling. But we don't enter those classrooms as blank canvasses. We receive our first educations from our cultures and institutions such as our families and religion. I had once believed that my early educations must be supplanted by those found in institutions of learning. But my *true* education came from constantly navigating ways of knowing and being that were assigned to me.

In my talk, I told stories to share some of the educations that I'd had: lessons on what it means to be a woman, on the proper way to be a Black person; lessons of silencing and learned self-censorship; lessons in how to erase oneself.

But truthfully, I wasn't interested in giving "the talk of my life." All I could do was go on that stage and be open and fragile and honest. I had *many* messages because my once-silenced stories were screaming to be heard. They deserved to be.

While writing my talk, I encountered a lot of advice: books, articles, videos. In them, I found common themes and rules on how to talk, tone, pacing, composure, posture, overcoming stage fright.

Something else those rules had in common? *They were not true to who I was.* But I wasn't selected to give someone else's talk; I was selected to give *mine.* So that is what I did.

Eight years have passed since my talk, and here is what I know: Not only do I have the right to take up space, but I am *fiercely* protective of the space I have claimed for myself. Living in this world in my Black, female body—without apology—is a radical act. Choosing to love and sustain myself while everything and everyone around me tries to change or diminish me is a revolutionary practice. I no longer offer myself so eagerly for others (or myself) to erase me. When someone tries to write the story of who I am, I no longer willingly hand them a pen.

What I was beginning to understand eight years ago—and wholeheartedly understand now—was that I could *not* have one central message, nor could I *ever* give the talk of my life. *Because still I live.* I am limitless. I am expansive. And I have more than one defining story.

Here are some of them.

I

Talk to Me Like a Black Girl!

Revision

When I was in my creative writing program, not once did I pretend to know what I was doing. Seeing me frantically walking the halls of the Humanities building or panicking while lesson planning in the computer lab was a common sight. I was overwhelmed, overworked, and felt that I was the only one stumbling in school, work, life. Everything.

Oh, and *nothing* prepared me for the experience of creating my thesis.

I had a brilliant thesis committee from whom I sought validation and an ambitious project I wanted to do justice. To my overwhelm, I added immense pressure to create the perfect text that would fulfill both of those goals. But when the time came for me to make revisions on my thesis, I felt...lost.

I *hated* revision. Throughout K-12 and my early college years, I would write one draft, submit it to the instructor, and get an A. In my later college years, I realized that the approach was not one I could continue. I resisted revision because not only had I never had to do it before, but I could not handle negative feedback or criticism in any form. I felt that the need for revision marked my work (and me) as a failure; I was supposed to get it right the first time.

I collected pages of comments and suggestions from my committee members. Sometimes I read their comments; sometimes I couldn't. How could I incorporate these bits of feedback, which sometimes disagreed with each other? I would sit and stare at a draft and just think: NO. I have NO idea how to improve the content. I have NO mental capacity for one more thing. I have NO physical energy.

So, I made a choice. A series of choices, really.

When I encountered a section, stanza, or paragraph that gave me trouble or that one of my committee members questioned, I deleted it if I wasn't immediately sure how to improve it.

Simple. Gone. And so, my pieces became increasingly shorter.

And that is how I survived my final quarter of graduate school: Delete.

* * *

29 August 2019

At some point in my youth, I decided that my role in life was to help other people toward greatness, with no regard to my own passions. There is something noble in supporting other people, sure, but not to the detriment of myself. I find myself 35 years old, and I have lived a life of standing behind and supporting from below other people—especially men. I will not do that anymore.

This life isn't working. I need a new one. Blow it up. Demolish.

* * *

On May 11, 2012, when I submitted my thesis to the Graduate School, I had no awareness that, approximately one year later, I would be standing on the stage of the campus Performing Arts Center. There, I would speak about how my struggle with a nonfiction assignment made me confront some brutal truths about myself.

The inaugural TEDxWWU, "Renovations: Building Our Future," was organized into two different sessions: "Self Renovations" and "Community Renovations." I was a speaker in the former.

In my application to speak at TEDx, I explained, in 100 words or less, what "Renovations" meant to me:

"Renovations" calls to mind buildings that, once pristine, over time became less so whether by human interference, disaster, or natural wear, and now need constant repair until in their best state. To renovate is not to destroy completely or demolish what once was, but to improve what already exists and add value. This is often true for people as well, who must constantly take on and try out ways of being and knowing, sometimes needing to replace or refine what's no longer functioning or productive—whether it's a long-held belief or behavior—until they are their authentic selves.

The person who wrote those words in 2013 seemed to know what she was talking about. She sounds so *sure*.

Of the pieces I have written, one of my favorites is a 383-word spoken word poem titled "The Grammar of We." It begins, "You were the only one / who could make me want / to break grammar rules on purpose." It's a poem about a straight-laced narrator who follows strict grammar conventions and the person they love and admire for their, as I put it, "grammatical deviancy." The narrator loves the other primarily because they teach her a novel way to engage with language—her *true* love. "The Grammar of We" is—at once—a love letter to a person and to language: the seductions of poetry, enjambed lines, anaphora. And then...the end of the poem and the love affair: "I lament that you left / you left without saying a word."

Any time I've performed "The Grammar of We," it's elicited laughter and memories of love, longing, and heartbreak from crowds. It's fun to perform, *slightly* sensual, and one of my more "lighthearted" pieces. I look at the genesis of "The Grammar of We," at the 33-word list of phrases and keywords scribbled in a notebook beginning "I want to kiss like you write."

I think of how this poem began its life and how it evolved.

Wow, this is so much better now. Look what you can do with just a few keywords and a sense of humor.

As a writer and former writing teacher, I cannot think of renovation without also thinking of revision. To take a piece of writing that's not *quite* working, analyze it, consider its many components, and then re-build from its foundation to create something new.

With revision, we look again, examine, reflect.

With revision, we start with the bones of something, then reimagine and refine.

No demolition necessary.

So, let's start with the bones.

Bones

I am standing in a hallway in the library, so I'm trying to keep my voice quiet. As the nurse speaks, I scribble on a purple sticky note.

avascular necrosis
Breakdown of bones + tissue
on both sides R worse than L
*Follow up Th, Feb 28th 11:30 am
**Orthopedist referral

Avascular necrosis? I hang up the phone and walk back to my office to consult the internet. I learn avascular necrosis also operates under a different name: osteonecrosis. I know root words. Osteo = bone, necro = death. The nurse didn't say "death," she said "breakdown."

Right now, I feel on the verge of both.

Text my boyfriend, Jonathan:

> Diagnosis from my doctor: avascular necrosis. They're going to refer me to an orthopedic doctor in Seattle. Sounds scary, and I'm kind of freaking out.

I send him a link to the article I read that says something about blood supply, tiny fractures in the bone, eventual collapse of the dying bones, and debilitating pain.

While I am deep in internet research, my friend and colleague arrives at my office for our scheduled meeting. I share that I have just received a diagnosis I am still trying to wrap my head around, which is why my face looks like it does. Depending on the situation, I sometimes choose to wear my emotions on my face. This is such a situation.

Somehow, I must work. I try to be present as she speaks, but one major question is lingering. A question I hadn't been able to read enough sources to answer: *What if, eventually, I won't be able to walk?*

Jonathan replies.

It certainly has a spooky name. You can have my bones!

* * *

It started with pain in my inner right thigh.

In July 2018, I had enrolled in a kickboxing class. I had a lot of rage I needed to channel somewhere.

I had tried crying; now was the time for punching and kicking.

I thought the injury originated from an overzealous series of round-house kicks to a heavy bag during class (again: rage). During my final kick of the combination, I realized too late that my technique was sloppy. Instead of kicking the bag with the bottom of my shin as my instructor had taught me, I kicked it with the top of my foot. It *hurt*.

The pain that I believed to originate from a muscle strain that would improve over a week or two instead worsens for weeks, approaching months.

When I take a step with my right leg, a sharp pain shoots through me, almost like a razor blade beneath my skin is slicing at my leg muscles.

Maybe it's not a muscle strain?

I visit my doctor in September 2018, and she refers me to physical therapy. I begin weekly physical therapy sessions. Get X-rays.

From: Doctor
To: Danielle
Date: 12/31/2018

The hip and pelvis X-rays you had show normal alignment, normal bones in the pelvis, and normal hip joints. So there is no evidence of arthritis or congenital (something you were born with) issues in the hips/pelvis. Keep working with physical therapy on the soft tissues, as I suspect that is where your pain originates.

I sit and read the email. I'd been attending physical therapy weekly from September 29th until December 29th in addition to completing the prescribed home exercises—all without much improvement. Seeing my co-pays stack up, rather than continuing with physical therapy appointments, I had decided to just do my exercises at home while waiting for the imaging results.

The pain has fluctuated. One week, I'd have pain off and on, but it was manageable. Other weeks, the pain was unrelenting. I eventually borrowed crutches from a friend so I could take some weight off my right leg.

Reading my doctor's email, everything in me thinks, *Do not let your pain continue without further investigation.*

I sit and contemplate how to phrase my dissent. I am still new to advocating for myself, but who will if I don't do it? I'm really not comfortable attending physical therapy indefinitely.

I begin a draft, then delete it. Close the email, come back to it. Repeat.

Almost one month passes.

* * *

From: Danielle
To: Doctor
Date: 1/25/2019

With regard to the imaging, even before the X-ray was ordered, my physical therapist said that an MRI would be better for diagnosis than an X-ray. I thought it'd be a few weeks until I was back to normal, but I didn't think it would be this long of a process, so I wonder if the extent of the injury is worse than I thought. I've been attending physical therapy since October, I believe, and if an MRI could better help identify the problem and inform treatment, I'd like to go that route.

After several drafts and with a rapidly beating heart, I hit "Send." Exhale.

From: Doctor
To: Danielle
Date: 1/30/2019

If your hip is not improved, I do think an MRI makes sense at this point. Insurance typically requires at least 6wks of PT without improvement—how many weeks of PT did you complete, and is it improved or worsened or the same at this time?

I write back and explain that I've completed a total of 13 weekly visits. My doctor submits an order for an MRI, and I wait.

2/4/2019

When I stand, I feel as though someone has taken shards of glass and is jabbing them into my lower back, hip, and down the entire length of my right leg. I troubleshoot and learn that if I bend my chest toward the ground and form a ninety-degree angle with my body, I reduce some of the pain. I move around my apartment this way, asking my furniture, counters, and anything else in sight to bear some of my body weight. This is precisely what I feared.

They're going to tell me I'll never walk again.

The MRI results arrive. The results weave a complicated tale.

What are you saying to me right now?! I read the report several times, annotating it as I look up unfamiliar words on an internet search.

Exam Date: 02/12/2019

MRI HIP RIGHT W/O

Clinical: Continued pain in spite of 4 months of conservative management and 13 weeks of PT.

Comparison: Pelvic radiographs from 12/27/2018.

Procedure: Standard MRI sequences were performed without IV contrast.

Findings:

There is bilateral avascular necrosis of the femoral heads.

On the right, geographic signal abnormalities involve the majority of the superior aspect of the femoral head articular surface with serpiginous low signal T1 and T2 abnormality surrounded by significant marrow edema that extends throughout the femoral neck to the intertrochanteric region. There is mild partial collapse of the anterior and superior aspects of the femoral head best appreciated on the sagittal right hip images, series 8 images 12 through 15. There is a 12 mm subchondral cystic focus at the anterior aspect of the femoral head.

There is a moderate-sized right hip effusion.

At the left hip, geographic signal abnormalities involving the majority of the superior aspect of the femoral head with serpiginous low signal T1 and T2 abnormalities surrounded by increased T2 signal intensity. No significant edema on the left involving the femoral neck or intertrochanteric regions. At the left hip, there is no effusion. No subchondral collapse of the left femoral head articular surface. No secondary osteoarthritic changes at the left hip joint.

IMPRESSION:

1. Bilateral avascular necrosis of the femoral heads right side worse than left involving the majority of the femoral head articular surfaces. On the right there is mild subchondral collapse of the anterior and superior aspects of the femoral head (stage IV Steinberg staging) with a moderate-sized hip effusion and significant marrow edema extending to the femoral neck and intertrochanteric region. On the left, there is no subchondral collapse (stage III Steinberg staging) or reactive marrow edema at the femoral neck.

So...not quite "normal alignment, normal bones in the pelvis, and normal hip joints," I suppose.

After I have completed reading the results for myself, I have two thoughts:

1. I feel so proud that I advocated for myself to get an MRI. Finally, I have answers for this pain.
2. The MRI has shown me something real. Now I must face something real.

February 28, 2019: The follow-up appointment

"I want to be sure that I answer all of your questions," my doctor says.

I've had the same doctor for almost six years now. She knows about my notebook and its list of questions.

28 February 2019

Q: *Why wasn't this condition noticed on the X-ray?*

A: *The X-ray may not be sensitive enough to detect*

Q: *Should I be concerned about blood flow issues elsewhere?*

A: *More likely to have this condition in other parts of body*

Possibly congenital > May refer to geneticist at UW (Seattle)

New prescription: Gabapentin > start @ low dose @ bedtime

Hold off on PT until treatment plan

No manual work/massage

TENS unit okay, pain relief

Light weight bearing/toe-touch weight bearing > both crutches

* 2-wheeled walker

We discuss treatment options, imaging other joints, blood tests for diagnostic reasons (lupus, sickle cell anemia, blood smear, metabolic panel). The doctor provides recommendations on pain management.

We try to discover how I might have this condition, review risk factors: Joint or bone trauma? (*Maybe the kickboxing?*) Related chronic medical conditions? (*Don't know*) Excessive alcohol use? (*No*) Long-term use of corticosteroid medicines? (*What are those? Oh. Then no.*).

I have none of the primary risk factors. Here, I learn a new word: *idiopathic*. It's a gorgeous, five-syllable word. I like the sound in this word, but I don't like what it means: a condition of unknown cause.

One day, I think my body is fine, and the next, I can barely walk.

Why is this happening to me?

Rheumatology referral. So many tests. Weeks pass. Then, results.

One or more of the antibodies associated with autoimmune rheumatic

disease is positive. Antibodies to Sm/RNP or RNP in the absence of
other antibodies is associated with Mixed Connective Tissue Disease.

Upon first being diagnosed with avascular necrosis, I had been afraid that my condition would degenerate so much that someday, I might permanently lose the ability to walk.

But after reading scores of health library entries for mixed connective tissue disease, my thoughts shift. More keywords and phrases: rare, cause unknown, no cure, can lead to life-threatening complications.

I am 35 years old.
What is happening with my body?
What else might I lose?

March 7, 2019

The surgeon walks into the exam room with a severe look on his face. He makes a professional introduction, then looks me in the eye in a way that is a bit too intense for my comfort.

"This is a serious condition."

He speaks, and I scribble.

There are four stages to classify the progression of avascular necrosis (AVN). My hip joints are at stages three and four for my left and right hip, respectively. Given the advanced nature of my condition, the surgeon suspects that for several months, if not years, my bones have been experiencing tissue death, and my hip joints have been collapsing —without my awareness. At these stages, other patients typically have greater difficulty standing and bearing weight on their hips and experience significant pain with any hip joint movements. He expresses surprise that I have only recently begun to feel pain. Considering my advanced staging, the surgeon offers the options:

Option 1) Have hip replacement surgery, which means removing the damaged cartilage and bone from the hip joint and replacing them with prosthetic components.

Option 2) Leave the condition untreated, which means it will worsen with time, leading to severe arthritis and loss of function.

Have surgery or live with excruciating pain and suffer.

So, he meant to say this: There is one option.

* * *

Everything is a blur. More internet research. Second (and third) opinions.

The other doctors too ask me about risk factors: Joint or bone trauma? (*Rage kickboxing?*) Related chronic medical conditions? (*You're the medical professional; you tell me*) Excessive alcohol use? (*Nope*) Long-term use of corticosteroid medicines? (*Not at all*).

Each time I answer "no" to their behavioral questions, I wonder if they doubt if I'm telling the truth.

After considering my "options," information I had gathered from some additional research, and the second (and third) opinions, I opt for surgery. I will make my foray into hip surgery as efficient as possible and have both surgeries done the same day: August 6, 2019.

What once was life is now appointments, labs, and paperwork. Several rounds of iron infusions to correct my anemia. Pre-surgery testing: complete blood count, basic metabolic panel, nasal swab to test for MRSA. With surgery day approaching, I learn that my iron infusions were insufficient to correct my chronic anemia, so I can't have both hips replaced at once, as the blood loss associated with two surgeries in one day would possibly be too significant. Disappointing. This health condition is seriously inconveniencing my life plans.

I decide to begin with my right hip because its condition is most advanced, though my left hip is hurting the worst at the moment. My second surgery will need to wait at least three months.

August 6, 2019

On the day of surgery, my mom sits with me in the pre-surgical waiting room. She reminds me that it's not too late to change my mind;

I can still seek another opinion. She's looking on her phone, and I can't tell for sure, but I'm pretty confident she's researching other options.

"Mom, we drove to the hospital...in Seattle. And we're now in the waiting room of the hospital. I'm having the surgery."

I don't remember much between when the nurse calls out my name to take me to my room and when the anesthesiologist approaches me with a syringe.

I wake up in a different room, with a nurse to my right telling me that I can expect to be cold, but the feeling will pass after the anesthesia wears off.

August 6, 2019

Had my surgery today. I'm feeling drugged, so I'm going to sleep now.

In addition to my journal, I brought a book, thinking that I'd read. I don't.

My fierce independence is not possible right now. During the hospital stay, so many rules to follow. Round-the-clock medication management. Every hour that I'm awake, I must use a breathing device called an incentive spirometer to encourage me to breathe deeply to avoid pneumonia. To avoid developing blood clots, I keep my leg elevated, complete leg exercises for circulation, and wear compression stockings. Everything is an instruction on how not to die from complications of surgery.

I have to push a button and call a CNA to assist me with the bedpan and eventually help me to and from the toilet.

My dignity, too, is unavailable.

A physical therapist comes to see me just hours after surgery and says we're going to get up and walk.

I'm sorry...You want me to do what?! Already? A surgeon just sawed off my femoral head!

If there were ever a time that I deserved to simply lie down, it is now. I just want to sleep. Rest the bones I still have and sleep.

Instead, I learn how to maneuver my body to get out of and into the hospital bed, sit down and stand up from the toilet, learn to walk.

As I am learning to use the two-wheeled walker for the first time, my mother stands a few feet ahead of me, clapping her hands as I take my first timid steps. I look down at the booties covering my feet and at my own hands that are clutching the grips on the bar of the walker. This walker looks like a less fun version of those push toys that babies use when they're learning to walk.

I look again at my mom's face as she cheers for me. She's so *proud*. Her eyes almost look as though they're remembering something.

"Oh, god...This is what it was like when I was a baby, and I started walking for the first time, isn't it?"

"Yeah, kind of!" she says.

We both laugh.

August 8, 2019

I demonstrate that I can walk up and down a set of stairs with crutches. I have final visits from the surgeon, the physician's assistant, nurse, and physical therapist. The after-visit summary informs me (in case I forgot) that I had been hospitalized for the arthroplasty hip anterior approach procedure due to femur head necrosis. My updated medication list and dosing schedule will help me manage all my medications. The instruction sheets and verbal directions tell me how to take care of myself at home and teach me how the implant changed my body and how to live with it. Upon discharge, the nurse advises me to schedule a follow-up appointment with my surgeon in one week.

Here's what you can do. Here's what you absolutely must not do. Here's what you can do if you can tolerate it. Increase activity as tolerated. Let pain be your guide. Maintain your pain medication schedule. Stay ahead of the pain, don't chase it. By the time you feel the pain, it's a bit too late.

Who were we?

Just before my 32nd birthday, I received a handwritten letter from a friend. In the days of "Happy Birthday!" text messages, his letter was notable not only because it was handwritten, but also due to the depth of thought he sent with it. He had written the letter after returning from a hike, during which he thought of me and had wrestled with some big questions.

Before society, religion, etc. got ahold of us, who were we? Before we knew we were black or that a certain grade of hair was considered "good," who were we?

– JONARAL KRISTOPHER,
1/23/2016

In the Beginning

Here is what I know. I was born in Los Angeles, CA on January 27, 1984. I join a family with a mother, father, brother, and two sisters.

The six of us live in South LA in a two-bedroom, one-bathroom pink house with white trim.

My early lessons:

1. You always say "please" and "thank you."
2. Look both ways before you cross the street.
3. You wash up before you eat.
4. You bless the food before each meal to thank God for the food.
5. When the ground shakes, stand in a doorway or hide beneath a table. When you hear gunshots, drop your body to the floor and do not get up until the shots stop.
6. You attend church on Sunday. You wear a dress to church. When you come home from church, you change out of your church clothes before playing.
7. Do not open the door to strangers.
8. Spare the rod, spoil the child. The rod (belt, house shoe, switch, comb, or hairbrush) hurts the parent more than it hurts the child.
9. You pay 10 percent of your money to the church. This is called a "tithe." It's for God.
10. Upon visiting anyone's home, you must speak to all present adults before you head off to play.
11. God created your body. Do not let anyone touch your body.

12. When you're in a store, always keep your hands visible.
13. "Keep your skirt down and your panties up!"
14. In school and (eventually) at your job, you will need to work twice as hard as other people.
15. Respect your elders. You do not talk back.

* * *

Here is what I know. My family moves to Moreno Valley, CA in December 1991. The six of us now live in a brand new five-bedroom, three-bathroom house with stairs, a fireplace, and a garage. When I first see the house, I say to my mom, "It's a mansion!"

More observations:

1. Most of the kids in my neighborhood and at school do not look like me.
2. My body looks different than my new friends' bodies.
3. My hair doesn't do what my new friends' hair does.
4. When I hear a *pop!* tear through what used to be silence, I don't pause to question: gunshot, backfire, or fireworks? I always assume gunshot.

I learn other things, too.

* * *

Accusation: I say the word "ask" funny. I say the word "ask" like "ax."
Source: A giggling friend.
Example: "I'll ax my mom if I can go to your sleepover."
Plan: Listen for when people like me say the word to confirm or deny.
Result: Confirm. "Ax."
Plan: Listen for when people unlike me say the word to confirm or deny.
Result: Confirm. "Ask."
Plan: Learn to say the word "ask" as my friend says it. Practice.

A Girl Who Loves Stories

Moreno Valley, CA: 1992

I sit cross-legged on the floor. So I don't accidentally show anybody my underwear, I make sure to tuck my skirt hem into the small gap where my shins meet. I fold my hands, place them in my lap, and wait. Storytime is my favorite!

Our teacher sits in a chair in front of us and begins reading from a book. I stare up at the teacher as she reads, *ooh* and *aah* at the pictures she shows us. Maybe it's our bodies huddled so closely together or my building excitement, but, after a few minutes, I begin to get hot. I tug at the neck of my sweater. I wish it were the kind with the buttons so I could maybe open it a little, but it's that evil type of sweater I have to pull over my head. I hate these. My head gets stuck in the hole, and sometimes not even my whole head—just my forehead and ear get caught in it, so my face is half in the sweater and half out and the fabric pulls at my eyelid. I want to take the sweater off, but I don't know if the white shirt I'm wearing underneath is the type of shirt you can show people who aren't in your family. My mom calls it an "undershirt," so maybe that means you only wear it *under* something? I don't know. I don't want to get in trouble, so I sit and try to pay attention.

Until.

A blond girl to my right pulls her sweater over her head, balls it up, and tucks it into her lap. I immediately look to the teacher for a re-action. I wait for her to say something to the girl, but she doesn't. *That girl's undershirt looks just like my undershirt! The undershirt must be okay.*

34

To be sure, I wait a few more minutes. The teacher continues reading, stopping every now and then to look at us and show us pictures. After another moment, I take a deep breath, grab my sweater from the bottom, and pull it over my head. On the first try. My head didn't even get caught! Just as I saw the girl do, I ball up my sweater and tuck it into my lap. *Ah.* My shoulders relax. I glance over at my twin. I wait for her to look at me so I can meet her eye and smile at her. Maybe she'll see that we're wearing the same shirt and want to be friends. I'm *so* excited about our matching white undershirts.

Until.

"I'm not going to continue reading the story until Danielle puts her sweater back on."

Oh no. No. No.

All eyes are on me. I look to my right at the girl whose actions I have copied. She is sitting cross-legged in her white undershirt with her sweater balled in her lap. Just like me. My eyes look from the girl, down to my chest, back at the girl, and then up at the teacher.

Wait…Does she *have to put her sweater back on? She's wearing the same thing that I am. Did the teacher not see that other girl? She's sitting only one person away from me, so the teacher* must *be able to see her too. Why am I the only one? What's different about us?*

Oh.

I'm new to the school, and I don't want to be the reason my classmates don't get to hear the rest of the story.

As the whole class continues to stare at me, I grab my sweater from my lap and pull it back over my head. My head doesn't get stuck this time either, though I kind of wish it did so I could hide. I keep my eyes fixed to my lap, in the space where my sweater used to be, now just my folded hands against the fabric of my skirt.

The teacher continues to read.

I don't recall the story the teacher read. But I definitely learned a lesson.

Scenes

...from a hallway
Moreno Valley, CA: mid 1990s

My family and I are visiting the home of my oldest sister's best friend. I am returning from the bathroom, and just as I am about to turn the corner from the hall to the living room, I hear it.

"The girl is too white!" the mother says, her voice an indictment.

I wait in the silence. I wait in this space for my parents to defend me. Instead, with their despondent "Yeah...," I am convicted.

Case closed.

The only one who speaks for me is the daughter—a teenager four years older than I, someone I barely know.

"You guys, she is *right there*. If I were her, I'd be crying right now."

Only then do I begin to cry.

...from the screen
Moreno Valley, CA: 1999

My friends and I have perfected the art of the chain letter. Even though we see each other every day at school, we regularly pass around chain letters by email that feature a list of probing questions. Here's how it works: the sender fills out their answers then sends the questionnaire for us to fill out and send along. These questionnaires almost always end with a promise if we comply with the instructions (Send this to 5 friends, and in 5 days your crush will ask you out!) and a consequence if we do not (If you don't send this message to 5 friends before midnight, someone you love will die tomorrow!).

Today's chain letter is from Megan, a girl I've been friends with since seventh grade. I read her answers. Pretty standard questions about celebrity crushes, favorite food, and trivia such as that. Then, I come to a question near the bottom about music.

Do you listen to rap or hip hop? *No, I don't listen to nigger music.*

I begin to have flashbacks.

Eighth-grade math class when a classmate would—as a "joke"—draw swastikas on my eraser and in the margins of my notebook paper that I had to turn in to the teacher at the end of class.

Sixth grade when I met a new friend and some of her first words to me were, "I can be friends with you, but I could never date a Black guy. My dad would kill me!"

White friends who claimed they were Blacker than I was because they knew some lyrics to rap songs that I didn't know.

I close my eyes, squeeze them shut, and open them again wondering if maybe I misread the sentence. But there it is, just as it was before. Black text on a white background.

Megan is a school friend that I hang out with every day. She, for some reason, felt it was appropriate to send *me* an email containing, perhaps, the world's most notorious racial slur. A racial slur that specifically targets Black people. Targets *me.*

I look at the list of recipients on the email. Megan has sent this message to our entire friend group, so everyone will see her words, and, with them, my name on the list of recipients: the only Black friend.

I consider Megan's email and think of the myriad ways she could have answered that question:

Do you listen to rap or hip hop? *No.*
Do you listen to rap or hip hop? *Nope!*

Do you listen to rap or hip hop? *No. I like alternative and ska.*
Do you listen to rap or hip hop? *No. Not into it.*
Do you listen to rap or hip hop? *Nah.*

But I'm glad she answered the question the way she did.
She has shown me who she is.

...*from a yard*

Compton, CA: 2000s

I am in the buffet line at a family gathering in my aunt's front yard when a man joins the line behind me. His body towers over me. I'm tall, but he's *tall*. Atop his dreadlocks sits a black crocheted cap with horizontal bands of vibrant green, gold, and red.

I look up at him and smile in the polite way I've learned to smile at adults I don't know. After all, we might be related. He introduces himself as an old family friend. I tell him my name and begin to explain my place within the family—

"Don't talk to me like a white girl! Talk to me like a Black girl!"

I am holding a large serving spoon in one shaking hand and a paper plate in the other. I don't know what to do with any of this.

I no longer have an appetite. I do not finish my sentence. I don't know any other way to talk.

This is the only voice that I have.

...*from the dance floor*

Des Moines, IA: 2013

My friends and I make our next stop during a bachelorette party bar crawl. We create a dance floor in the middle of the venue as the other patrons drink at the bar along the wall. As has been the case all evening, I am the only Black person in the establishment.

As I dance, a blond woman shimmies her way to me with intention.

I know what is about to happen; I have been a character in this story before.

Charge: "Come on, sista! You can do better than that!"
Processing: My body deactivates dance mode.
Lesson: Black people have a limited catalogue of approved dance moves. I have violated a social rule.
Conclusion: Reject.
Assessment: "Nope. I honestly can't," I say. Also, I am most certainly *not* your sista.
Processing: My body reactivates dance mode.

...*from an office*
Bellingham, WA: 2012

My professor tells me that a story I have written reminds her of Jamaica Kincaid.

"Have you ever read her work?" she asks. I have not.

The energy shifts in the room. I realize I have given the wrong answer.

She begins listing off names of other writers; I take notes. All the names are of Black, female writers.

Audit of the room: 1 white, female professor. 1 Black, female me.

She turns to her bookcase, pulls texts from her collection, and hands them to me. With each book that passes from her hands to mine, I almost hear the authors' voices speak through the spines: *Girl, we were here this whole time. Where were you?*

I sit with the growing stack of books in my lap, my notebook and the notes I have written beneath.

Jamaica Kincaid. Gwendolyn Bennett. Rita Dove. Lucille Clifton.

So many others.

I have graduated from high school and two institutions of higher education. I have one quarter remaining of graduate school. And yet.

Not until my comprehensive exams in the summer and this very moment have I ever met them.

I haven't read these authors. My education never gave them to me. But I also didn't look for them.

...*from everywhere*
Any Place: Any Year

"Why do you talk like that?"

"Hey, why you talk like a white girl?"

"What, you think you white or somethin'?"

...*from a car*
Bellingham, WA: 2011

I have offered to give a new friend a ride to Bible study. We listen to pop music, and I sing along.

"Can you dance Black for me sometime?" she asks.

Different week. Same person. Same destination.

"Can you wear your hair natural for me sometime so I can see what it looks like?" she asks, running her hand over my crown of flat twists.

...*from a bar*
Bellingham, WA: May 2011

A man tells me he loves my skin.

We exchange names: *Danielle. Nabil.*

The headliner for tonight's show is Champagne Champagne, a hip-hop group from Seattle.

Nabil's voice competes with the band's enthusiastic set, but the accent I hear in his voice roots my feet to the ground.

"Where are you from?" I ask.

"Bellingham!"

"No...where are you *from*?" I ask, with different emphasis and absolutely no right.

"Morocco!" Nabil says, continues, "Where are you from?"

"Southern California," I respond. I look down to stir the ice in my glass. I know the question he will ask me, and I dread it.

"Where is your *family* from?"

"I don't know, exactly...Isn't that terrible?" I look out at the dance floor, continue, "Somewhere..."

"Africa, yes? I am African, too!"

He rubs a hand down my arm.

"Beautiful! I love Black skin! See? We have the same skin!"

"No, not quite. I think mine is a bit darker," I say with a laugh. Everything he says is an exclamation point.

Nabil buys me a whiskey sour, and for this, I let him tell me again that he thinks I am beautiful.

Perhaps it was my fault. Maybe I led him on. After all, it was my touch that began this interaction. I had placed my hand on his shoulder as I approached the bar where he stood, asked, "You don't mind that I'm touching you, do you?"

I don't know why I did it. Maybe the marriage of music and liquor.

Earlier in their set, Champagne Champagne performed a song called "Magnetic Blackness." Maybe that's what it is.

I thank Nabil for the whiskey sour, but I return to the dance floor alone. I need space to dance.

...from downtown
Bellingham, WA: 2013

The featured poet for the evening is a popular writer and educator from Oakland, CA. After the open mic, a handful of us leaves the café for an impromptu after-party. The introvert in me is aching to go home and curl up in my blanket, but I am so enamored of the poet and her work, so I stay.

As the others carry on conversations, I walk alone in the street behind them. I take some quiet time whenever I can get it. In my mind, I practice some potential conversations that might happen at the party, so I'm not entirely unprepared for social interactions. Though I'm a frequent presence at the weekly open mic, I don't really know anyone.

I've been deep in silent conversations with myself, so I don't hear the reason why we've stopped at a restaurant. In the lobby, our group stands in silence and waits.

One of the group members whom I've never seen before breaks the silence, apropos of nothing. We assume our roles.

White Male: "I don't think I have enough Black friends."

Black Featured Poet: "I can't...."

[Black Featured Poet leaves the lobby and walks outside.]

Black Me: "I don't think you can ever have enough Black friends."

White Male: "..."

Later that evening, I say goodbye to the Black Featured Poet before she travels back home to Oakland or the next stop on her tour. She gives me her number so we can stay connected. I text her so she'll have my number too.

My Black Text: "Can I be your Black friend?"

Her Black Text: "Nope. Already reached my quota!"

...from the banquet table
Bellingham, WA: 2013, 2014

At the African Caribbean Club Heritage Dinner, the students proudly wave the flags of their home countries: Eritrea, Ethiopia, Kenya, Nigeria.

More flags and countries than I can track.

I sit at the table, with my folded hands shielding my face. Tears travel down my arms.

I don't know which flag I would wave.

A Space Between

CW: Body image disturbance, disordered eating

Liminal. I heard the word thrown around a lot in our graduate school classes. It was a word I pretended to understand. Then, even, I suspected some of my peers didn't understand the word either. We were graduate students, after all. Impostor syndrome, I suppose.

How jarring to be not Black enough in most spaces but to represent Blackness in others.

For the first time, I think I begin to understand.

* * *

In some spaces, I am praised for how much of me exists.

I am 14 when a male classmate tells me, "You have thick thighs, but I like 'em like that." I did not ask. Nor do I reply. Not directly. My answer sounds like no more food eaten that day, 300 crunches after volleyball practice, standing on a scale wondering how much my vital organs weigh and how to account for them.

"Girl, those full thighs are our culture. Embrace those hips, baby." An unsolicited comment on a picture of me in my volleyball uniform. With that, I am on the scale for the fourth time that day. My response sounds like kneeling on a bathroom floor. I speak draped over a toilet bowl.

In some spaces, I am praised for how little of me exists.

My family moved me to the predominately white suburb one month before my eighth birthday. I noticed immediately how different I was.

But I waited until I was 10 years old to begin my first diet. I had joined the pep squad and saw how different I looked in my skirt compared to the other members. When required to wear my uniform to school, I would tie a sweater around my waist to hide as much of my flesh as possible.

Living in my body amongst other girls, I felt like I was conducting an informal ethnographic study. I collected data from my peers and mass media—the usual suspect—and presented this data in the form of an eating disorder.

My tiny waist, my enviable six-pack abs, my slender arms, my thigh gap: This is what the data told me I should want. So I wanted it.

And I got it.

* * *

Before I moved to Bellingham, WA, I read about the weather. About how Bellingham often tops the list of cities in the U.S. with the least amount of sunshine. *I can probably handle that*, I thought.

Before I moved to Bellingham, WA, I read the demographics. About how Bellingham's Black population was 1.3 percent (of nearly 81,000 people), while the campus where I would be studying and teaching fared *slightly* better at about 2 percent (of approximately 15,000 students). *I can probably handle that*, I thought.

In both cases, I soon found that reading about it is different than living it.

Before I moved to Bellingham, WA, I didn't realize two things: (1) how much the lack of sunshine would affect me, and (2) how much the lack of Black people would affect me.

As a lifelong resident of Southern California, I was well aware of how important sunshine was to me. As a lifelong Black person, I was not aware of how important Blackness was to me.

I could somewhat address my seasonal affective disorder and vitamin

D deficiency by taking supplements and sitting in front of the light therapy lamp in the student union building.

There was not such an easy solution for the other deficit.

Though I moved to Bellingham in pursuit of a graduate degree, I sometimes joke that my most significant education was in the development of my Black identity.

I could not hide in Bellingham; I was "the other" or "the only" in most rooms I was in, and people were eager to remind me as such. With so few Black people around, I became a model of what a Black person was. But here, dissimilar to my experience back home, most of the response wasn't as much "You aren't Black enough" as it was "Perform Blackness for me." There was one commonality, however.

As a resident of this in-between space, everyone around me felt entitled to enforce my adherence to *their* understanding of Blackness. The way my body looked and moved didn't belong to me. The expression of my emotions—from joy to anger—didn't belong to me. My voice didn't belong to me.

* * *

After watching my TEDx Talk, some family members confessed to me that they hadn't always been proud of their Black identity, either. I would love to say that I handled those confessions well, but I didn't. Instead, I was angry.

Why, then, did you make me feel that I was the only person who ever had shame about this? Why did you not say to me, "We were taught to hate ourselves, and I didn't escape it either"? Why make constant remarks about the way I talk? Where was the lesson that I had accepted a flawed narrative that my Blackness made me inferior? That I learned to think in terms of deficit because I was taught to think in terms of deficit? That I had assumed responsibility for something I didn't need to carry? That I could seek an alternative narrative? Where were the patient, compassionate discussions with me?

If only someone had said, "The shame you feel is not your fault. Your Blackness is not a problem; the problem is the *story* that others have created about your Blackness."

Welcome Home

From Danielle to Kim
July 14, 2013

I need to tell you something. I apologize in advance if I ramble.

When I found out the verdict, I was at happy hour with some of the girls from the Black Student Union, and I am so happy that I was with them when I heard it (I'm really glad that I've found this little community up here, but that's a story for another time). After I dropped one of them off at home, I stopped by Matt's place because he lives across the street from her. This was around 12:30 this morning, but he wasn't in. He called me this morning at 7:30 because he saw my missed call. We spoke for a little, and I told him that I had come over because I was upset and needed a hug. He asked why, and I said, "Because of the verdict in the Trayvon Martin case." And he asked what the verdict was. He had heard that a verdict was in but didn't know that G.Z. was found not guilty. It boggles my mind that you can hear that a verdict was reached in this trial and not even be, at the very least, curious enough to find out what it was.

After we hung up, I tried to take a nap, but I couldn't stop crying. I went over to his place this afternoon because I was sobbing and needed to be held. He asked me to tell him what I was feeling. This just made me feel worse, and I hated him being next to me, even as he tried to be a comfort to me. As I was leaving, he said, "I'm sorry you're feeling down." *I'm sorry you're feeling down.* I know that he was just trying to comfort me, but I just burst into tears in my car. It's not about feeling down. You know this. He can read about the case, recommend to me articles to read about it. He can even, perhaps, sympathize. But he can never empathize. He will never be able to know.

Now, you know I've struggled for a long time being comfortable with being Black; you saw it long ago, even though I've only admitted to it in the last few years. Part of why I got so angry was not because he is unable to empathize, but it's because I expected him to. I didn't want to have to explain any of this to him. And I realized it's my own fault because I'm the one who hasn't been attracted to Black men to the same degree as I have been to others. I have been so blind in so many ways.

I don't even know where I'm going with this. I guess I'm writing because I want to thank you for how you have, over the years, called me out on my own internalized racism and self-hatred. Undoing more than 2 decades of this mentality is not going to be easy or quick, and I've been struggling with doing so, especially since I've started to pull my head up out of the sand these last few years and have started to pay attention. I admire your strength, and I just wanted to tell you that you're one of the people that I really look up to.

* * *

From Kim to Danielle
July 14, 2013

Danielle, PLEASE hear me on this: You have no reason to be ashamed of a mentality that has been ingrained in us for generations. We've been made to feel inferior for hundreds of years so you being a victim of it is not a unique experience. ALL OF US have felt it at some point in our lives. I'm just lucky to have had parents that had lived thru Jim Crow and had been thru too much shit to allow me to fall permanently in the shame hole.

I respect you SO much for realizing your truth, owning up to it, and actively trying to change it. Most of us STILL have ourselves in chains, and the sad part is they will never even know they're chained because they never try to move. I am so deeply proud of you. You are not the girl I met several years ago (I loved her too), but you have grown into an amazingly smart woman who is humble enough to admit that you weren't always proud to be Black. That's a hard thing to admit to yourself. I never had your strength because proudness was forced upon me at an early age. I had no choice then. You are CHOOSING to be proud in a world that constantly tells you otherwise, and that is the real strength. I remember trying to plant seeds in your mind because I could recognize that you were just misguided. It was always out of love.

And about your boyfriend, you're right. He'll never really get it. Just like my White Aunt, Uncle & cousins will never really get it. I'm sure Matt meant well, but it's a whole different experience when you grow up never having to defend or even think about your race on a daily basis. I'm sure he has never woken up and thought, "I'm White," yet hardly a day goes by that we don't have to be conscious of our Blackness. From the way we interact with people, the way we talk at work/school, the way we carry ourselves, the way we wear our hair, what clothes we wear, what music we listen to in public, what we eat (don't be caught eating fried chicken, watermelon, or drinking Kool-Aid or grape soda), we constantly have to make sure we're not making anyone uncomfortable with our Blackness. White people generally don't have this issue.

You can't blame yourself for only being attracted to White men because you weren't really loving yourself, so how could you love a Black man who is an extension of you? It was all a part of a schema that you viewed the world from, a schema that was created generations ago, so how can you be at fault? Now that you see the world and yourself for what you really are, now the task is yours. Continue to make your strides and vow to yourself that you will never crawl back into that shame hole. Leave your shame and regrets in that hole, bury them, and never look back. Your hatred for yourself is in the past, and your old denial of your Blackness never removed you from our family. You still are and will always be a part of us. Welcome home, sista. I love you. I respect you. I am PROUD of you.

A Long Time Comin'

CW: *Mentions racialized violence and murder*

I am listening to soul music. A relative of mine walks in and hears me singing along.

"When did you stop being ashamed of your Black identity?" she asks.

Can I just listen to Sam Cooke without interrogation?

I have no coherent narrative for you. I can't tell you when I first began to recognize that I needed to address the person I was *before*. What I can tell you is that there is no *after*. There is only *during*.

Here is some of what was possible for me *during*.

In November 2012, I begin a job at Western Washington University's Ethnic Student Center. On my first day, I meet with the Dean who oversees this department and several others. She is a Black woman. She tells me I am the first Black woman to ever work in the Ethnic Student Center. I have the job description that lists my responsibilities and salary and the orientation packet that outlines my health benefits and retirement plan. With the Dean's words, I feel I also have a new assignment.

In my role, a small percentage of my job description is to be a historian and archivist. I learn the history of the Center that began with student activism in the mid to late 1960s when the students of color on campus demanded a space. Their call would not be answered until 1991. On

Christmas Day 2012, I write an email to a friend and share about my new job:

> I'm working on this huge archiving project right now, trying to set up an archiving system for all of their records and historical documents —everything from pictures, VHS, cassette tapes, newspaper articles, etc. This is the part that I'm so excited for. I'm reading the history of the center from the mid to late '60s when the students of color on campus were trying to get the center started. Honestly, I've cried several times reading some of those documents because I literally have their history in my fingers. It's such a weird, crazy feeling. I've Googled some of the names of the early students and found that they're now politicians and lawyers and professors, and I feel that I've walked into the best history lesson a girl could ever ask for.

I serve on the planning committee for the annual Women of Color Empowerment Dinner. I coordinate the Women of Color Empowerment Scholarship and read the applications of young women who embody a pride in self that I ache for even now. In my first year of managing the Ethnic Student Center Conference, a student writes me a note: "*Thank you for the opportunity to make friends.*" I produce the inaugural Ethnic Student Center Commencement and watch students tearfully express gratitude to their families for simultaneously being the reason they exist and the cause for which they labor. The students in the Black Student Union ask me to be their advisor.

On December 4, 2014, student organizers stage a die-in protest in response to the death of Michael Brown at the hands of a white police officer. Though it's Michael Brown's recent death that provoked the action, there have been *so* many others. The organizers read the names of Black people who have been murdered in acts of racialized violence. With each name read, participants choose when to lie down on the ground. I don't remember which name brought my knees to the bricks. Some lie down for four and a half minutes—a gesture to symbolize the nearly four and a half hours Michael Brown's body lay dead in the street while detectives investigated the scene. Some of us lie down longer as rain obscures the tears on our faces.

A 19-year-old student sits quietly in a chair in the corner of my office. Other days, he would drop by, sit down in the chair, and crack jokes, always the very picture of charm and exuberance. But not today. Another Black male has been murdered for daring to exist. I sit and hold space for him as he says, "It doesn't matter how many degrees I get. All anyone will ever see is just another Black dude."

A student writes me a card: *"Thank you for helping me to grow as a Black woman."*

There are other things.

* * *

When did you stop being ashamed of your Black identity?
Once, I overheard a conversation between this same family member and another—both Black women. These two women had, over the course of my life, openly criticized me for the manifestations of my internalized oppression. On this occasion, the two women were looking at a picture of a model in a magazine, who was a dark-skinned Black woman. The women couldn't believe that the dark-skinned Black woman was a model in earnest or that magazines would want to feature her because of the darkness of her skin.

"They're making fun of her," one of the women said.
How interesting, I thought. *You didn't escape it either.*
I know that—if I am not careful—I could easily fall back into shame. I must be vigilant. I must decide every day that I will accept and love myself because anti-Black racism and its messengers persist. I cannot try to exist in a space called *after*.
There is only *during*.

II

Smart for a (Black) Girl

Admission

If I don't select this box, am I denying who I am?

The "Demographics" page of the application asks me to describe my ethnic background. The supplemental text assures me that providing my demographic information will not affect my chances of admission; the university collects demographic information solely for statistical purposes. I do not know if I believe this.

I look at the "African American or Black" box.

I consider my classmates and future employers. I had heard the stories of people like me accused of "stealing" a spot at a top college because of affirmative action. The assumption was that this other person deserved the spot, and the "affirmative action admit" did not. Would they say, "Oh, well, you *know* she only got into that college because she's Black"?

I know my track record, my accomplishments, and my perfectionism. I know what the percentiles and standardized test scores say.

She only got into that college because she's Black.

Would I need to present evidence to defend myself?

Evidence: I was a student in the Middle College High School (MCHS) program. For the last two years of high school, I'd completed all my coursework at the local community college, simultaneously completing my high school graduation requirements and a curriculum to transfer to a university.

Evidence: Despite a *minor*, ongoing mental health crisis, I graduated with a 3.78 college GPA, completed my associate degree in humanities & fine arts with great distinction, and received a certificate of achievement at the MCHS graduation ceremony for completing the program with the highest college GPA.

Evidence: I can provide a writing sample. I can provide references from the teachers who told me I was bright and said they expected great things from me one day.

What would be enough?

She only got into that college because she's Black.

Though I would discern the prejudice and the lie in those words, a small part of me would wonder if their accusation was true.

I decide to leave the box blank. The question is optional, after all.

* * *

Spring arrives. While at my job at the music box shop in the mall, I receive a call from my dad.

"A letter from Berkeley arrived. Do you want me to open it?"

My heart pounds. Following what I've seen on TV and in movies, I ask, "Is the envelope big or small?!" Big means you got in; a small envelope means you didn't. He says words. No manner of description of this envelope will suffice. I wish I were at home so I could see it. Why did the letter come now?! I've been checking the mail frantically every day.

Hmmm. If I didn't get in, I don't want to break down on the phone with my dad or while at work. What's in this envelope that my dad cannot definitively state is big or small? Waitlist, maybe? Or a rejection with a list of other things I should consider doing with my life other than college?

I'm too curious to wait, so I let him open it.

From his side of the phone: "Dear Danielle, I am pleased to offer you admission to the University of California, Berkeley. Your application to the College of Letters and Science has been approved for the fall semester 2003."

From my side of the phone: I hear, "Dear Danielle, I am pleased to," and I draw in a breath and hold it. "Offer you admission to," and I clutch my chest. "The University of California, Berkeley," and I stifle a scream in the middle of the store as I burst into a dance. I hear no other words.

* * *

Berkeley has been my dream school—the school I have talked about incessantly—since I learned what college *was*. I had first read about Berkeley's rich history of involvement in social and political movements. But then I learned of its stellar reputation of academic excellence, and I felt a longing to be with others like me who sought a rigorous, intellectual environment. In sixth grade, I wrote an essay that declared, *"I want to go to Berkeley and study computers."* My dream then was to be a graphic designer; I just didn't have the language to know what I wanted. I didn't even know if Berkeley had a graphic design program in 1996 when I wrote that essay. All I knew was that I liked playing on my family's computer and drawing pictures in Microsoft Paint. And I knew that Berkeley was where I wanted to draw my pictures.

The letters continue to roll in. I am accepted into every college to which I applied.

However, the choice is really only between Berkeley and UCLA.

To my surprise and the surprise of everyone who knows me, I decline admission to Berkeley and enroll at UCLA. To myself and to everyone who will listen, I explain my decision.

Let me translate that for you:

She says: "Berkeley is on the semester system, and I prefer quarters."
Translation: "I am terrified to wander too far from home."

She says: "Berkeley has an English Literature program, and I really want to focus on American Literature."
Translation: "What if I get to my dream school, and I'm not good enough for my dream?"

Gestures

Immortalized in my fourth-grade yearbook, there is a picture of me wearing a white dress, ruffled socks, sponge roller bangs, and shame. In my hands, I hold a participant ribbon. My head lowered and my gaze fixed on the ground. And though you can't see them, tears are drowning my face. The camera missed them; my memory does not. To my left, my then-friend Alesha is looking at me, undoubtedly, to see if I was okay. I wasn't.

* * *

Peering out in the dark auditorium, I fix my eyes on the very center of my mom's face. As I stand on stage illuminated by spotlights, the only way I can stay calm is to look at my mother.

The Fifth Annual Rainbow Ridge Elementary School Spelling Bee: January 20, 1994. Exactly one week before my tenth birthday.

The judge gives me my word, and I spell.

The way I learn that I have misspelled the word is—partway through spelling—I watch my mother lower her head into her hand and shake her head: no. With this gesture, I understand my loss before the judge tells me that I am wrong and to please exit the stage.

The auditorium fills with my gasping sobs.

Throughout the remainder of the spelling bee, I sit staring at my lap, crying. When the photographer calls the participants to the stage for the group photo, I am still crying.

After the spelling bee ends, I climb into the rear of my family's minivan because the bench seat faces the back of the van. Typically, this is where I would sit with my siblings as we made funny facial expressions and gestures at cars and passersby. Tonight, in this rear-facing seat, I learn to cry silently. I learn to shield my face. I will not be able to see the disappointment on my parents' faces.

On the way home, my parents stop at the grocery store and tell me I can get any treat I want, and I don't have to share with my siblings. Even in my current state, I recognize the significance of this moment. As the baby of the family, I often receive hand-me-downs.

I get to choose my own thing.

But what thing? My parents trailing behind, I walk through the aisles and consider my options. Candy? Ice cream? Chips? It has to be the *right* thing. I walk down the various aisles more than once.

And then I spy a jar of dry roasted Planters peanuts. I recognize the peanut guy from the TV commercials. *These are the thing.*

My parents and I walk to the checkout while I stare at the glass jar in my hands, admiring the peanut wearing a top hat. I climb back into the rear of our van, where I immediately resume crying. Clutching the glass jar, I shovel peanuts into my mouth between shuddering cries.

During the drive, I cry with my entire body. I can't wait to get home to run to my bedroom and continue crying with my head under the blanket. My dad stops the van at a stoplight.

Are we almost home? I look up from my lap, and a cry catches in my throat. There, in the car behind us, is a woman. My shoulders settle. My head tilts to the left, left ear almost touching my shoulder. I partially lower my eyelids so I can focus more on her face.

The woman is crying, too!

After a few seconds, the woman looks in my direction, and we lock eyes. In a movement barely perceptible, she chuckles, her shoulders rising then falling. The woman wipes tears from her face with her left hand, and then she raises her right hand with her palm facing me, fingers spreading slightly. For a few moments, her hand remains suspended, then she returns it to the steering wheel, where her left hand is now at rest.

In my mind, thoughts are racing:

She *couldn't* be gesturing to me. I'm not going to wave because maybe her hand just twitched, and what if I wave and look stupid?

But...What if she *is* waving to me?

Why is she crying? What could have made this woman so sad? Will she be okay? Does she have a mom who will later hold her and tell her she'll be okay?

I decide that I don't care that I might look stupid. I can wave at her; it's fine.

As soon as I build up the courage to raise my hand to gesture, the light turns green, and my father drives forward through the intersection.

Away from the woman, her gaze, and my chance to be brave.

The Keychain

There were times when I was not so shy.

In elementary school, when I liked a boy, I made sure he knew. He knew, and *everybody* knew. My favorite way to express my devotion was to gift the boys poems I wrote about them. When the boys would try to put my declarations of love in their pockets or backpacks to read later, I would say, "No! You have to read it *now!*" and stand in front of them as they read the poem on the spot.

For some reason, I never had any luck with boys.

I was a very attentive student. Teachers loved me because I enjoyed answering their questions and offering my insights. While other students goofed off, I would listen with rapt attention, pen or pencil in hand, waiting for the next time to learn something.

"You know, Danielle, boys don't really like smart girls," a friend said to me one day after class in fifth grade.

What? That's dumb. Smart is the best thing. That doesn't make any sense.

"Wait...really?!"

Oh, that's why. I had been taking the wrong approach all along. Maybe I was too smart, and I intimidated the boys.

I would try a different approach.

One evening, my sister showed me a keychain she bought at the mall: IF IT WEREN'T FOR BOYS, I'D QUIT SCHOOL

Oh, wow. I asked to borrow it for a day. I loved school, but I thought the keychain would get me attention, maybe cause a few laughs.

The next day at school, I strutted around, swinging the keychain on the strap of my backpack. As my friends and I were heading to recess, I called them to the closet where we kept our backpacks to make sure none of them missed seeing the keychain. I made a big show of it.

Too much of a show. My antics caught Ms. Cagle's attention.

Ms. Cagle was a strict woman who wore glasses that covered almost half of her face and a perpetual "Don't you test me today!" look. Of the three fifth-grade teachers at our school, she would not have been my first choice. I was terrified of her.

I suppose when a teacher sees a group of girls huddled in a corner, she suspects they're up to something. We were up to something.

Ms. Cagle looked into the circle and saw that I was holding out the keychain. She picked it up, and as she held the keychain in her hand, I felt my face burn. She looked down at it, then rose her head to fix her eyes on me, glaring at me behind her large glasses. *Oh no.*

"Miss Smith, I'd like a word with you," she said and then dismissed the other girls to recess.

When she turned her back to walk to her desk, I looked at my friends and rolled my eyes. *Girls, go ahead without me while I deal with this inconvenience.*

Inside: *Oh no. Oh no. Oh no.* I did not like getting in trouble.

She grabbed the keychain on my backpack and held it in front of my face.

"What is this?" Not a question; an accusation.

I started crying immediately. Between gasps and tears, I managed to say, "I don't know! It's stupid! It's not even mine; I just borrowed it from my sister!"

"Is this why you haven't spoken up in class lately?" Though she asked the question, she didn't wait for an answer. She didn't need to.

"Don't bring this back to school. And I expect to hear from you again, Miss Smith."

"Ok."

She dismissed me to recess. I wiped my tears and joined my friends on the playground.

Stupid keychain.

May I have your attention, please?

It is sudden death spelling bee. Some bravery had found me, and, following my crushing defeat last year, I decided to compete again.

In the final round of the competition, my good friend Jenee and I, the remaining participants, have been alternating—each spelling our words correctly in turns. Then, Jenee misspells her word.

If I spell the next word correctly, I win glory! Hundreds of people will chant my name! Widespread fame throughout the school.

Okay...maybe just Ms. Cagle's fifth-grade classroom. *Tens* of people will shower me with praise and know I am a word champion.

* * *

During the intermission of the school's annual spelling bee, the pep squad always performs. Thus, a spelling bee competitor who is also a pep squad member has a choice to make. There would not be enough time to change clothes during intermission. The pep squad member could choose to wear the uniform and stand in front of an auditorium full of people on a stage and spell words in a short skirt.

Or what I chose.

During the performance, there were about 20 girls wearing blue pleated skirts and the school pride t-shirt. And then there was one squad member about six inches taller than the rest wearing an ankle-length dress. Doing dance choreography and high kicks and turns in slippery dress shoes.

Other girls may have decided to simply wear their uniform during the spelling bee. But me? With these thighs? Not a chance.

I didn't want to call attention to myself.

* * *

The word is "lurid." I do not know this word. I spell it just as it sounds: "*Lurid...L.*" Okay, that's easy. Pretty sure there's a "*U.*" "Lurid" sounds something like "lure," so there's probably an "*R*" next. The end sounds like the ending of "lid," so... "*I*" and then "*D. Lurid?*"

I do not endeavor to feign confidence in this word. I guessed, and everyone knows it.

But I am right. And I am now Rainbow Ridge Elementary School's spelling bee winner! Finally, I have won the trophy with the gold-plated bee holding up its forefinger: First Place.

The next day, during morning announcements, Ms. Cagle fixes her gaze on me.

Oh no. Please don't.

"I have one final announcement. Last night, Rainbow Ridge held its annual spelling bee—"

I sink lower in my chair.

"and the winner was your classmate—"

I sink lower until my head disappears into my desk.

"Danielle Smith. Let's all give her a round of applause."

As Ms. Cagle announces the victory I had said I wanted, I hide and pretend to search through my desk while she and my classmates clap for me.

As school champion, I have earned the right to compete in the district spelling bee, but I decline. I tell everyone who will listen that I just don't want to compete. I am bored of studying words and want to focus on something else.

I even manage to convince myself somewhat that this is true.

Lesson. Plan.

In middle school, a classmate tells me that he is surprised to see me in *his* advanced math class because he finds me attractive.

Him: "I didn't know pretty girls could be smart."
Lesson: Attractive girls cannot be smart. Therefore, smart girls are not attractive.
Flashback: Ms. Cagle's fifth-grade classroom. "I expect to hear from you again, Miss Smith."
Plan: He and *our* advanced math class will hear from Miss Smith again and again and again.

Like

In the UCLA catalogue, I read every entry in the Curricula and Courses section because I don't want to accidentally miss studying something I don't even know exists. I read each entry in full—from African Studies to World Arts and Cultures.

Quite a few majors interest me. Anthropology! Comparative Literature! Psychology! Sociology! Oh, but there is one that truly excites me. I read the section again and again and think *Yes, this is the one.*

I select American Literature & Culture. American Literature & Culture was not the one.

* * *

A few weeks after fall quarter begins at UCLA, I walk into a program office and tell them I want to change my major; I want to declare Women's Studies. *This is the one.*

When I read the entry—the penultimate entry in the catalogue—I knew I wanted to major in Women's Studies. I felt it in my bones. But there was a voice that gave me pause. *What will I do with that? I need a more practical major, I guess.* So, naturally, I chose to study Literature.

Sitting in the Women's Studies program office, I feel at home. *This is where I will find my people.* The student affairs officer asks why I want to declare the Women's Studies major.

I say lots of words, my excitement tumbling out of me so fast I almost run out of breath.

"Like! Like!" She chuckles.

I stop talking. Assess.

Of the myriad words I've said, she has heard the word "like" the loudest.

I sit in the office, in a space that has a purported commitment to uplifting women's experiences and voices.

Et tu, Women's Studies?

From this encounter, I collect two lessons:

1. As with much of my life, *what* I say is not important, but *how* I say it matters. There are additional ways that others will judge the way I talk.

2. Consciously limit the use of the word "like" when I speak.

You're SO articulate!

WOM STD 130: Women of Color in the U.S.
Spring 2004
4 credits

Course Aims: Examine the experiences of women of color to assess the intersections of race, ethnicity, class, and gender.

Experience: During class discussion, a classmate comments that our fellow Bruins consistently make assumptions about them because of their ethnicity and gender.

Facts: (1) My classmate is Black; (2) my classmate is male; (3) my classmate has an athletic build; (4) UCLA is a competitive university, a Public Ivy, and is often ranked among the best universities in the world. Therefore, students who are accepted into UCLA are commonly understood to be excellent scholars and up to the task of the academic rigor awaiting them; and (5) UCLA has an outstanding football team.

Analysis: My Black, male classmate with an athletic build is a student at UCLA. Therefore, this Black, athletic male plays on the football team.

Assessment: Each time, the Black male replies, "No. Actually, I'm here because I'm smart."

Observation: What an *excellent* comeback.

COURSE GRADE: A

So, tell me about yourself.

I am 21 years old and deeply concerned about how little I am prepared for anything. Having recently abandoned my recently acquired dream as a lawyer ("I'll just be a yoga instructor"), I have no idea what I want to do with myself.

What I know for sure is that Sallie Mae will expect me to pay my college loans after my rapidly approaching six-month grace period ends.

Another thing I know for sure is that most articles I've read assure me that I have no so-called "marketable skills." Though I *do* have an education I've been cultivating far from the campuses of educational institutions—what our society has coined "soft" skills. Listening. Communication. Creativity. Work ethic.

So, with my newly earned bachelor's degree, I walk into a staffing agency in search of "marketable skills." After taking some skills tests and sitting for a brief interview with a recruiter, I am deemed not entirely incompetent and am added to the payroll.

One day, the staffing agency calls me and says they have a job lead for me...in Norco.

Ooh...Norco?

A mere 30 miles from where I have spent the past fourteen years growing up, Norco seems like a different world. Nestled in a primarily liberal state, Norco's conservatism is demonstrated not only in its politics but also in its very fabric. Downtown, the pavement markings in the center of the main road are painted red, white, and blue. True to its federally trademarked nickname "Horsetown USA," Norco is an equestrian-oriented community. The city council has strict architecture mandates for all buildings to preserve the Western identity for which Norco is known and celebrated. The town has horse crossings featuring distinct crosswalk buttons: one at standard height for pedestrians and another a few feet above for people on horseback. Where other cities have sidewalks, Norco has equestrian trails. People ride their horses through the Starbucks drive-thru. To some, Norco is heaven.

The few times I have visited Norco, most of the locals glared at me. *How did you gain entrance to our heaven?*

I have deep reservations, but I am also broke, 21 years old, and living at home with my parents.

"Sure. I'll go," I say.

The next morning, I drive to the address the recruiter gave me, park my car in the dirt lot next to a horse corral, then walk into the building. I survey the room. In case I had forgotten I was in Horsetown USA, every inch of this lobby—from the chairs to the artwork—would surely remind me. There's an animal skull mounted on the wall next to me.

I take a few deep breaths and smooth my hands down my skirt. *I am an employable professional.* I recall the keywords in my rehearsed answer to the "So, tell me about yourself" question I was told is inevitable. Remember the firmness of the handshake my mom helped me practice.

When I turn the corner into an open office area, I am greeted—and I use this term generously—by a man wearing a cowboy hat. He does not rise from the table. We do not shake hands. He leans back in his chair then gestures to the chair opposite him at the desk.

I sit. Smooth my skirt. Fold my hands in my lap. Sit up straight. This is how I was taught I am supposed to look in an interview. Pleasant. Agreeable. Composed.

He puts his feet up on his desk. Cowboy boots. I do not react. I had learned some time ago that to survive some social situations, I would need to control my face and not let my emotions betray me. Stoic.

He sits this way for the rest of what is essentially a one-way interview.

He asks a couple of generic questions, but I mostly offer details about myself and my experience. *Answer with a pleasant look on your face. Smile.* I can see my résumé on his desk, but he hasn't looked at it once.

The clock on the wall over his shoulder tells me I have been in this office for less than 10 minutes. In this time, I have determined I have no interest in working here. I gather *he* has no interest in my working here. But I am professional, and I complete tasks that I start. If nothing else, I can consider this practice for future interviews. More soft skills.

Finally, he leans forward slightly toward his desk, picks up a corner of my résumé, and looks at it briefly.

"UCLA. Huh. That's a good school. How'd you get in there?" He puts my résumé down and looks back at me.

Over the years, when people learn I graduated from UCLA, I've received many reactions:

Oh, wow. Good for you! That's a great school.

That's a difficult school to get into. You must be really smart.

I'm jealous. That was my first choice, but I didn't get in.

Oh, that's my daughter's dream school. I should have her talk to you.

Go 'head, girl!

Not one "*How'd you get in there?*" Not once. Not ever.

How'd you get in there?

I know this one. I, after all, am a UCLA graduate. I have developed the critical reasoning and analytical skills as promised to me in the college catalogue. *Tone?* Accusatory. *Body language?* Dismissive, bordering on hostile. *Intention?* Genuine curiosity not detected.

How'd you get in there?

"Well, clearly, I'm very intelligent," I say, leaning back into my chair, fixing my face into a sly grin, and staring him directly in the eye.

This is how a Black girl talks.

He chuckles, pulls his feet from his desk, and stands up.

I stand up too, thank him for his time, and walk out the door.

Truly. Excellent. Comeback.

Transcript

CW: Depression

When I become an educator, I tell my students about my educational journey.

I keep my college transcripts in my desk so I can share them when I am in advising appointments with students whose stories are similar to my own. When I teach classes, I display my transcripts on the projector and share my story with my students as an exercise to teach about the value of accessing campus resources.

Reviewing my Riverside Community College transcript, I tell them how you can see my evolution. You can see my foundation begin to crack.

* * *

Fall 2001

Description: I'm standing in the MCHS program office, reviewing my recent transcript.

    ENG-1B Critical Thinking & Writing Grade: A
    MAT-10 Precalculus Grade: A
    SPA-1 Spanish 1 Grade: A

As expected. But among the expected, I see a grade that does not exist in my universe.

"What?! What is this?!"

POL-1 American Government Grade: B

This must be a clerical error. I don't get Bs; I get As!
My cumulative GPA has plummeted from a perfect 4.0000 to an unacceptable 3.9412! I turn around and walk to the desk of the program assistant. I shove the transcript in her face.
"How do I get this erased from my record?!"

CUMULATIVE GPA: 3.9412
President's Honor List

* * *

MAT-1A: Calculus I
Spring 2002
4 units

Description: What you don't see on my transcript are the other two classes I had been enrolled in this semester because I dropped them before the withdrawal deadline. I didn't want to be a doctor anymore.

COURSE GRADE: C

* * *

PHS-1: Introduction to Physical Science
Fall 2002
3 units

Description: I'm sitting in the back row of my Intro to Physical Science class. The hood of my sweatshirt is pulled over my head, and I am crying, hoping no one sees me.

Why don't I understand this?

The professor's notes on the chalkboard just look like a random assortment of shapes. Looking around me, all of the other students seem to understand these shapes. It's the third week of class, and I'm completely lost. For the first time, I feel stupid.

I can't breathe.

I pack up my stuff and walk out of class. I find a payphone, and—

[Yes, a payphone. That's how old I am; this is before I had a cell phone. This is 2002, so y'all were, what, like five years old or something?]

Anyway, I call my MCHS counselor.

"I'm never gonna become a doctor! I'm a failure!"

I'm full-on crying in a phone booth while students are playing hacky sack on a lawn next to me.

My counselor tells me to breathe. I breathe.

"You are *not* a failure," he says, then says more words that I don't remember. He asks if I've considered talking to the professor or getting tutoring.

No and no. *I don't get tutoring; I am a tutor! I tutor other people.* Other people *need help, not me.*

After talking with him for several more minutes, I stop crying, and I've calmed down a bit. He convinces me that it's okay to drop a class and to not finish something that I start.

Before we hang up, he repeats, "You are *not* a failure."

I immediately walk to Admissions & Records and drop Intro to Physical Science.

COURSE GRADE: W

* * *

> ENG-9: Introduction to Shakespeare
> Spring 2003
> 3 units

Description: I hadn't been attending class, but I would show up to the classroom at the end of each class period to submit my work. I had just accepted admission to UCLA, and I didn't want to risk my GPA. This time, when my English professor sees me peeking through the classroom window, she stops her lecture and steps into the hallway. She asks me to meet with her after class is over. We meet in her office.

"So, tell me what's going on," she says.

I immediately start crying.

"I'm so depressed!" I somehow manage to say.

More crying.

I tell her about what every day looks like. I just want to sleep, but I know I have to leave the house, or my family will be suspicious. I find the strength to get out of bed, get ready, and drive. I tell her how I leave home every day with the intention to go to class, but I can't quite make it. Sometimes I drive to a park. Sometimes I drive to an empty parking lot. Once I land, I sit in my car and cry or just feel nothing. Sometimes I arrive on campus. I park in the parking lot and try to gather the energy to get out of my car, but it's like my legs can't move. I've already dropped half of my classes and am barely surviving the other two.

She says she understands; her father lived with depression, so she knows how crippling it can be. She encourages me to seek counseling. Did I know there was a Counseling Center on campus? No, I didn't. She shows me the section on the syllabus where she had included information about campus resources, including the Counseling Center. [So, as I've said before, always read your syllabus.]

That's great, but what I *really* need to know is if I'm going to fail. UCLA, you know?

"No. My syllabus doesn't consider attendance in the calculation of the final grade, but if it did, I could fail you."

Relief.

"When you are here, you are brilliant. But you need to show up to class."

So, after that, I show up to class.

COURSE GRADE: B

* * *

GRADUATION

Cumulative GPA: 3.7850

Associates in Arts Degree Awarded on 06/2003

Humanities & Fine Arts

GD – Great Distinction

---

* * *

Qualitative Data

Administrators are concerned about students' mental health. The data show that student mental health crises are on the rise.

I have my own data. I look at my students' faces, read their assignment responses, am told directly in advising appointments.

At the start of class meetings, I do check-ins, either verbally or by handing out index cards, on which students respond to prompts. One day in fall 2015, the week before finals was particularly challenging.

1) *What's the state of your well-being today?*

Stressed. Exhausted. Tired. Worried. Not really motivated. Anxious. Overwhelmed. Nervous. I've been depressed and stressed. I am more stressed than I've ever been.

2) What do you need?

Sleep; Need to rest and relax and not freak out; Need a vacation, sleep, and my bed; I want to go on a walk, maybe by the water, to just breathe and not think; I need to go on an adventure and spend time with people that I love and who love me; I just need to remind myself of the good; I need a little time for myself. I have been working really hard, so I feel like I haven't had any time for me; I need to not be so attached to my boyfriend. I need to get my own space too; I need someone to socialize with; I just need to find a place to live and then take a nice, long nap after I pass my math final; I need a place to feel comfortable in because I don't feel it here in Bellingham or WWU (not really a fan).

The students look around them and think: *I'm the only one.*

* * *

Students are not satisfied with platitudes, generic statements, or statistics from administrators. They are not fooled by the brochures or banner ads displaying smiling students wearing spirit gear.

They want honest, real stories.

Students look to the front of the classroom or across the desk and see professors and administrators who appear composed and confident and have a collection of credentials after their names.

Q: How could this person ever understand what I'm going through? They've never been there.

A: So many of us have been there. I *live* here.

Quarter after quarter, I have honest, real conversations with my classes and advisees. Students' gratitude comes in myriad ways. Comments on teaching evaluations, but cards, letters, and drawings, too.

I could tell you really cared for us and our education.

I enjoyed having a teacher that reinforced the value of a student-teacher relationship.

I really liked how Danielle really understood us. Because as new students, not knowing what to do, she was there for us.

The teacher's ability to connect with the students made the class enjoyable.

I really liked the introspective approach and building a community.

I think your experience and insight was beneficial in a sense that you are reinforcing the class to go out and seek help, be organized and don't give up and stuff. You're the nicest teacher I've met since kindergarten and I really respect my time in class here.

I loved the class. Especially because it inspired me to do things out of my comfort zone. Thank you for being patient! Hope to see you often.

Danielle's overall attitude and passion for teaching was obvious in her commitment level and diligence for helping students.

She was a great teacher and overall I can tell she loves what she does.

I think Danielle was an inspirational instructor who is very open to people's opinions. I enjoyed this class because I could express my thoughts and feelings!

♥ *you. Thank you for caring.*

Danielle is very inspirational, and I will miss being in her class.

I want to say thank you for making my first quarter in college a great experience. I want to apologize for not actively contributing to the conversation often, but I do appreciate the safe environment you created within our class. I'm so thankful that you were our instructor. Thank you for encouraging us to stand up for ourselves, our wants, and our dreams.

Qualified

CW: References self-harm, suicidal ideation, and mental health disorders

"Did you see the scars on her arm?" Michaela asks quietly after the student leaves the office.

Michaela's still in training, so she's required to have a more experienced advisor observe her appointments.

Yes, I had seen them. The arm with the tattoo.

"That doesn't surprise me," I say.

Michaela looks puzzled. Asks me to clarify.

"I've read that some people who have a history of self-harm sometimes get recovery tattoos to cover their scars," I say.

* * *

My left forearm bears a tattoo of a cross sitting above the text II Corinthians IV: VIII-IX. My right forearm reads, "We are hard pressed, but not crushed"—the first part of the verse. As my tattoos are so visible, people often ask me about them.

Recently, while I was in the finance office signing documents for my new car, the finance manager asked what the verse says.

"We are hard pressed on every side, but not crushed; perplexed, but not in despair; persecuted, but not abandoned; struck down, but not destroyed."

"That's deep...What's that mean to you?"

"I got it in a visible place so I can look at it and remind myself to keep going."

"Damn…You really been through some stuff, huh?"

Yeah, you might say I've been through some stuff.

When I got my tattoos done in 2008, I didn't know about the practice of recovery tattoos; the placement of my tattoo was just a coincidence.

* * *

The students I advise and teach have been through some stuff.

The girl in Michaela's office felt especially familiar. I know the system: the checklists, the color-coordinated planner, The Plan.

These are the students who often escape notice. They don't raise the "at risk" flag on early alert systems. They are not the "academically underprepared" who are extensively assessed.

Educators praise their GPA, send them congratulatory emails lauding their presence on the President's Honor List, and offer them entrance into Honors cohorts.

I am a highly sensitive person working in higher education. I am also forthcoming with my life's stories. As a result, my colleagues often want to refer students to me, saying: "I just think you'd be a good person for her to talk to," or "I thought they might connect with you." My colleagues are usually right.

Just as I recoil at job postings that list "high stress tolerance" as a required qualification, I don't want to become well qualified to interact with trauma. This is not a skill I want to cultivate.

I've been told I'm naïve, silly even, because I dare hope for a world that demands much less from us. A world that doesn't subject us to such a rigorous training program for positions we didn't apply for. A person who has high trauma tolerance is a person who has been tasked with—and has been forced to adapt to—too much.

The students want to be heard, so I listen. I listen as they disclose their diagnoses of depression, anxiety, ADHD. Listen as they express suicidal ideation, which then means I walk with them to the Counseling Center down the hall, to someone more qualified than I am. Then I walk back to my office alone, wondering if I'll ever see them again.

The students want to be seen, so I see them. The students who show up with scars—physical, emotional, and otherwise—without knowing how fresh the scars or whether the existing ones will be their last.

Student Life

"She's very strong in language, and though not as strong in math, she's up there," the educators say.

Regularly, my standardized test scores for reading and writing are around the 97th percentile or higher. My lowest score is in math, which is usually a percentile in the high 70s or low 80s.

The school curriculum comes easy, and I rarely have to work hard to do well. I am assessed for and accepted into the Gifted and Talented Education program at Rainbow Ridge Elementary School.

My 99% on a test—the highest in my class—elicits a "Why isn't it 100? Where's your other percent?" from my father.

Early, the story I tell myself is this:

1) Failure is not an option.

2) I must achieve and maintain perfection, or my parents will not love me.

* * *

In December 2008, when I was hired at UC Riverside in the Department of Student Life, what became apparent to me was that my single-mindedness had caused me to miss out on exactly that: a student life.

Since I was a child, I knew intimately how to be a scholar.

During my first visit to the Moreno Valley Public Library, I asked the librarian the maximum number of books I could check out at one time. Each visit, I'd get a towering stack of books and carry them to the counter. And though I had weeks to complete them, I consumed the books, finishing with them well before the due date. I begged my mom to let me go back to the library; I was there almost every week. At home, for fun, I read my family's Encyclopedia Britannica collection. I loved learning. I wanted to know *everything*.

* * *

After winning the spelling bee in fifth grade, I didn't claim my rightful place in the district spelling bee because I was too afraid to fail.

I had also begun to feel an immense amount of pressure that robbed me of the joy that learning once brought. I began to hate words because there was no longer simply excitement, but expectation.

After a while, school began to have one purpose: a high grade point average.

Because I had built my sense of self around being a perfect student, although I graduated with a solid academic record from a well-respected university, I didn't know who I was apart from being a student. If I were to be honest, I would say that I likely began working at a university because I was terrified to leave the site of academia that constructed me—or so I believed.

Eighteen years, one bachelor's degree, and one master's degree later, I still have the acceptance of admission from Berkeley—the blue folio holding my acceptance letter, dated May 1, 2003. The letter that began "Dear Danielle, I am pleased to...." The letter telling me to listen to the sound of the world opening at my feet. The learning opportunities I will find nowhere else. I kept the letter because I couldn't throw it away. That blue folio was validation that I was good enough for Berkeley.

Good enough.

* * *

At UC Riverside, I worked with the student programming board to plan programs and events for the campus. I was 24 years old, just a few years older than the student employees. While I had spent my college years in an unbalanced pursuit of academic perfection, I observed the board complete feats I thought were impossible. They were emerging as activists and serving communities both local and global, traveling abroad for study and pleasure, creating art. In their student leadership roles, they were greatly respected for their dedication to serving the student body's needs. All of this *while* excelling academically.

I watched as the board steadily crafted aspirations they knew they had the potential to achieve. In seeing how impassioned they were, I realized that I had never pursued my own passions—namely, writing. I had done what was safe; the board showed me what was possible.

Writing has always been my way to explore, understand, and examine life. Writing is how I speak. What a tragedy then that something so vital to me would be withheld from me *by* me.

I walked the world with my hands covering my mouth.

The board knew how deeply I lamented this unfulfilled pursuit, and they urged me to take the steps toward it. To start, I would apply to creative writing graduate programs. As many of them also prepared for graduate school, they cheered me on as I studied for the GRE on lunch breaks, reviewing material that had been pushed out of mind for nearly a decade.

In the spring, we received acceptance and rejection notices—celebrating the wins and breathing together through the disappointments.

There were no concrete interactions or moments with the board that changed my life, but the sum of my experiences in the 22 months I worked with them.

The board gave me the confidence to pry my hands from my own mouth.

* * *

In September 2010, I quit my job, packed up whatever items fit in Bridget Jones (my Suzuki Aerio), drove roughly 1,400 miles north to a town where I knew no one, and traded my highest salary to date and full health benefits for a teaching stipend that placed me below the poverty line.

Though irrational, the move was necessary for my survival. I *needed* to study creative writing. If not the best decision I've ever made, it certainly is near the top of the list.

In choosing this life, I finally allowed myself to pursue what I desired rather than simply ache for it. I devoted myself to writing with the goal to simply love the experience of writing. The master's degree I earned as a result of that experience was just that—the result but not the purpose. The experience allowed me to—amongst many other things—discover my voice and the courage to use it.

Then, I began to create a definition of myself that relied not on the institution of education but on my own merits. Within my reach, a robust life that I had finally given myself permission to build.

In 2014, my poem "Song for My Beloved I: Loving" was published in a literary journal alongside one of my long-time heroes whose textbook I studied as a Women's Studies undergrad. When I saw her name on the list of contributors, my mouth fell open.

"Cherríe Moraga?! Cherríe '*This Bridge Called My Back*' Moraga?! Is this real life?"

I held the book open in my hands as tears rolled down my face and landed on the page. The page that held both our names.

A life like this was possible all along. I simply took the risk, then, to believe I deserved to live it.

I wish I could tell you that I moved through life with confidence from that day forward. I want to tell you that I never again shrank from attention. I would love to tell you that insecurity and fear of failure were lost on me.

But let's be honest: There are too many pages remaining in this book for that to be what happened.

* * *

Early in my higher education career, a visiting speaker at a campus event spoke to student leaders about self-efficacy, or the belief in one's own ability to accomplish difficult tasks, achieve a goal, and overcome challenges. He especially grabbed my attention when he stated that people who are low in self-efficacy at times "self-select" out of success.

The presentation was for students, but I, the alleged student affairs professional, was taking notes. He explained that despite evidence that might suggest a likelihood of success—such as a record of achievement —our own limiting beliefs *about* our abilities can cause us to opt out of pursuing opportunities or to create obstacles that could prevent us from realizing our aspirations.

A 10-year-old choosing not to compete at the district spelling bee. A 19-year-old saying no to her dream university. A 26-year-old, broke graduate student who almost declines a paid teaching assistantship because she's terrified to stand in front of a classroom. A 29-year-old writer who—when offered the opportunity to be the featured poet at the open mic she frequents—says, "I'll think about it" and then proceeds to think about it (a lot) but never follows up. A 29-year-old woman who almost drops out of speaking at TEDx.

My goal after graduate school was to pursue a career as a writing teacher or become an editor and writer. Instead, five months after graduation, I found myself returning to work in student affairs at the university from which I earned my graduate degree.

I had done it again. I had done what was safe.

I continued to erase myself.

School Girl

That's the name some of my classmates at Angeles Mesa Elementary School called me. "School Girl" was not a compliment. "School Girl" was a label I was supposed to be ashamed to bear.

School Girl read the books, completed the assignments, answered the teacher's questions. These behaviors made School Girl uncool.

School Girl never graduated.

* * *

This week, while reading an article in an academic journal, I encountered a sentence marked with an asterisk (*). Instinctively, I looked to the bottom of the page for a footnote. None. I looked at the References section at the end of the article. Nothing. I thoroughly searched the document and its pages, but I found *no* mention of why this text had an asterisk next to it. *Why is there an asterisk here?!*

In common usage, when a writer marks a word or clause with an asterisk, this signals that they will provide further information, details, or context in a reference, footnote, or comment. We also see the asterisk in advertisements to point the audience to the fine print, which often takes the form of a disclaimer or terms and conditions.

Writer, why have you decided to ruin my afternoon?! All I ask is that you provide me with the information you promised to provide me. Instead, you have flouted asterisk usage rules with no regard for my feelings. Worse, there is knowledge somewhere I can't access!

Perhaps others would not be as bothered by a punctuation mark so carelessly attached to a word or clause without explanation. But me? I *need* to know. I'm not allowed to not know things.

* * *

One evening while I was in my early 30s, I had an anxiety attack and *slight* meltdown because I realized that—in my lifetime—I will not be able to read every book I will ever want to read. It's just not possible. There isn't enough time. I consider my curiosity one of my best traits, but I have somehow become unable to *sit with* curiosity. I can't simply *remain* curious. Almost as soon as I have the thought "I wonder...," I am already researching the answer. I don't allow myself to wonder.

I constantly feel the ache to be a student of *something.* In the past year alone, I have considered getting an MBA, attending culinary school, moving to Paris to study in a French language immersion program, becoming a certified financial planner, completing a user experience design immersive program, applying to graduate programs in data science and instructional design, and attending a hospitality management program in Switzerland.

Each time, I reign myself in. I first asked, "What are you running from?" After a while, the question evolved into "What are you seeking?"

I thought I had determined that my worth and value weren't found in intellection, striving, and achievement. Hadn't I learned that these ways of being and doing were not who I am but solely what I have historically done and performed?

I recognize this. *Learn more. Know more. Enter this program of study and there you will find yourself and your validation.*

When it's 2:13 am on a Wednesday, and I'm filling out a contact form to request a curriculum guide from yet another program, I have started reminding myself that what I want to do is write, as I have wanted for my entire life. Not to be a data scientist. Writing is the only interest that has remained constant in my life, so I know I can trust this desire. After all, what am I when you strip away a learned behavior that ties my self-worth to what I know and achieve?

I am a girl who loves words.

Critics

"I want you to stop apologizing for your work."

In my second quarter of graduate school, I took a course on writing short prose. After a round of workshop, my brilliant professor wrote these words across the top of my draft.

What? Apologizing for my work? After class, I asked her to explain.

She informed me that, each time I offered a piece of writing for workshop, I said, "I'm sorry. This is the best I could do," or "I wish it were better."

Guilty. She forgot to mention "I just threw this together." I *never* just threw anything together. In fact, I worked very hard on my writing. But if I set expectations low, when my classmates inevitably told me I was a fraud and ran me out of the classroom, their disappointment would be warranted. *No bother. I just threw this together in 60 minutes.* On the other hand, if my classmates read my draft and believed I just created this masterpiece in the 60 minutes before class, they would herald me as a creative genius.

Neither of these things happened.

* * *

As a child, I hid away with my journals and books. I didn't like to raise my voice or be noticed. I was cripplingly shy. Anytime someone paid me any attention, I'd wonder why.

I never thought I was worthy of being seen; however, I thought everyone was always looking at me, judging me, and waiting for me to fail.

As I walked through my elementary school lunchroom looking for a place to sit, I imagined every student was looking at me saying, "Look at that loser who has no friends." While that could certainly be true (kids can be assholes), what's more likely is that they were just eating their lunches and talking to their friends or deep within their own minds and insecurities that they didn't have space to consider me, let alone judge me.

I simultaneously thought I was invisible and too visible, not important and the center of the universe.

* * *

Submitting a piece of writing for workshop was one of the most terrifying and vulnerable acts of my life. A piece of myself laid bare on a page offered to other people. And I had to sit with all attention on me and listen to my classmates and professor pore over my words. I would sit in my chair and feel actual physical pain. Every part of my body that had the ability to clench *clenched*.

I wore discomfort like a second skin. During my first workshop in the short prose class, a classmate leaned across the table, placed her hand on my arm, looked me squarely in the eye, and said, "Thank you for trusting us with your work."

Sharing your writing for critique by your peers and professor is the primary activity in creative writing class meetings. So, I had to show up and be vulnerable *repeatedly*. Once again, I felt like the kid in the cafeteria holding my lunch tray. But instead of just walking quietly through the lunchroom, all of the students in the lunchroom *were* actually looking at me, and they could read my mind.

* * *

Toward the end of my Women's Studies program, my Violence Against Women professor reminded the students in the course that our privilege of higher education also bore a responsibility. She asked each of us how we would use our knowledge to change the world.

"By writing," I answered when my turn came.

There was one minor complication. How would I change the world by writing if I kept almost everything I've written to myself? Even though I've always been a prolific writer, I was too scared to share any work that I had written. One of the first times I had done so was when I applied to graduate school and submitted a writing sample.

I soon realized that if I didn't become comfortable with workshop, the next two years of graduate school would be unbearable.

It is not personal. The point is for your writing to get better.

Over time, I began to show up in workshop a little less afraid. When I handed out my drafts to the class, I began to catch myself before I apologized for my work, often saying nothing at all. I would listen as my professors and peers provided feedback. Take some and leave some.

Not only did my writing improve, but I survived. Imagine that.

* * *

In creative writing classes, you learn to review and critique others' writing in workshops, and, in the process, you cultivate the skills to do the same with your own writing.

The goal of *any* educational program is to equip you with skills and knowledge sufficient for you to carry the lessons with you outside of the learning environment.

This is the importance of understanding all the educations that we've had and the teachers that provided them—those with degrees and those without. Whose lessons do we carry with us?

In my TEDx Talk, I mentioned how I had developed a narrow understanding of what an education is. When asked what encouraged me to pursue higher education, I said that I instinctively knew that I was destined to go to college. At hearing this, my mom was compelled to *gently* remind me, "No! *I* gave you your first education." She then proceeded to school me by recounting the ways she did exactly that. I had no retort; my only possible response was to acknowledge my own ignorance. In my mind, education meant a building, someone with credentials. I am the first in my family to earn a bachelor's degree and master's degree. Though my family members don't have post-nominal letters after their names as I do, they are both students and teachers of their own educations.

Whether or not we are aware of or acknowledge all the educations that we have, they teach us regardless. From the useful lessons that teach us how to live in the world to the destructive lessons that work tirelessly to diminish us that we unfortunately internalize.

There are the formal lessons: Kids, here is what it means to Black in this world. As Christians, this is what we believe and how we behave. This is what's appropriate to talk about and what isn't. Girls, you're getting older and developing now, so here is what to do (and not do) with your body.

And the informal, often unspoken ones we learn through observation: This is how power dynamics operate in our family. Respect the hierarchy of the family unit. This is how relationships function (or don't).

When we are exposed to a curriculum that promotes inferiority and self-doubt, we carry it with us. We no longer need additional lessons or external messaging; we assume the role of the critic.

I was a sponge of these familial and societal lessons (after all, I was an excellent student). I have always been a fan of learning.

Unlearning, on the other hand, is new. What serves me and what doesn't? What nourishes me? What depletes me?

What do I delete?

* * *

"You walk this world with gentleness."

My dear friend Elena whom I love and deeply admire said these words to me, and I hold her words among the most beautiful compliments I have ever received. For most of my life, I have been chastised or dismissed for being "soft." Too sensitive. Too quiet. Too introspective. Elena was one of the first people to tell me that my natural ways of being were not defects.

I never believed these traits of mine were flaws to overcome.

As a child, when I would cry, my elders would say to me, "Stop crying, or I'll give you something to cry about!"

I have already identified a reason to cry; that's why I'm crying.

The generous part of me wants to believe that this approach was an attempt to build resilience in me. Another lesson for how to live in a dysfunctional world. But I didn't want to be taught to adjust to dysfunction. If the world indeed operates the way I have been taught, if life is truly hard, and humans are in fact increasingly callous, then we need *more* sensitivity, not less. An additive approach, not a subtractive one. A narrative that says, "Keep your sensitivity but also learn resilience."

As an empath, I can often read and absorb the emotions in a room, read body language and tone. I observe people and situations more than I speak. This way of being is likely why I noticed George in our classroom that day and made the life-altering decision to talk to him.

Being an empath is, at once, what helps me walk this world with gentleness and what makes walking with gentleness in this world sometimes completely unbearable.

* * *

How would I change the world?

I had felt that my answer was small in comparison to others' answers. The concept of changing the world feels very grand. What really happens, I believe, is that these changes are granular.

As I had discovered with my student's words "You're the first Black teacher I've ever had," my mere *presence* in a room changed someone's world. What if I had succumbed to fear and declined the teaching assistantship, and she never saw me standing in front of her classroom? How much more education would she experience before she ever had a teacher who looked like her?

For me, changing the world may look like diverting another writer away from the path of self-criticism. Or sharing vulnerable, honest stories that make others clear their throats before they share a truth they've never told. Being a model for someone to learn that they can effect change even if they doubt their own voice, even if they get nervous when they speak, even if they need to speak with a script and a podium.

Elena—whom I and many others know as "Dr. P"—died in September 2017 at 67 years old. At times, I speak of her in present tense because I believe that she walks (and dances) this world with me still. With her passing, I choose to honor her by holding ever more fiercely to the quality she saw in me.

You walk this world with gentleness.

If gentleness is how I walk the world, maybe that's how I'll change it too.

III

Will You Take This, Woman?

Content Note

Some of the chapters in this section reference violence and sexualized violence. I use the term "sexualized violence" to encompass forms of violence that are perpetrated through sexual conduct. Numerous studies show that the primary motivation for perpetrators who commit these forms of violence is not to express sexual desire, but to exert dominance, power, and control. Sexualized violence assumes many forms (e.g., physical, psychological) and includes a spectrum of contact and behavior, including (but not limited to) sexual harassment and sexual assault.

* * *

RESOURCES

In the back of this book, I have compiled a selective, but not exhaustive, list of organizations that offer direct services for survivors and provide education programs and initiatives to eradicate sexualized violence.

Call and Response

As a child, I attended church whether I wanted to or not. My mother was (and still is) a devout Christian and strongly believed in raising her children in the church.

When I had aged out of "children's church," I was required to sit in the main congregation. In protest, instead of listening to the pastor's sermon, I would replay television episodes in my head or flip through the pages of the Bible for stories to read.

I soon found that the Bible contains poetry and...erotica?!

An entire book of erotica somehow snuck into the holy text of my mother's faith. *Does she know this is in here?!* I cast a furtive look at my mother before I continued to read.

Song of Songs (also known as Song of Solomon) is a book that is subject to multiple interpretations. The most common interpretation within the Christian faith is that Song of Songs is an allegory of Christ and the Church, his bride.

Erotica. Allegory. Call it what you want.

Song of Songs intrigued me because—as an erotic text nestled in a holy one—its presence was almost defiant. This quality is what captured my interest initially and what kept my attention throughout my teenage years and graduate school.

For the last section of my graduate thesis, I wrote a series of "call and response" pieces to Song of Songs—one for each of its eight chapters. I titled my responses "Songs for My Beloved." Here, I share the first in the series, "Song for My Beloved I: Loving."

The "Beloved" of my texts also defies straightforward interpretation.

Song for My Beloved
I: Loving

Do not stare at me because I am dark,
for the sun has gazed on me

– SONG OF SONGS 1:6

I. ANECDOTE

It's time for revision in Race and Ethnic Relations. *The name of this paper should be "Interracial Marriage,"* the Black sociology professor corrects. The seasoning is off. Too bland. "Intermarriage: Love in Black and White" has a better mouthfeel.

A. LECTURE NOTES
Professor: *Black couples do not engage in public displays of affection to the same degree as do white couples.*

Lips. *I don't accept it*, mine say.
Lips. *Young lady, you're arguing with many years of research*, scold hers.

1. EVIDENCE
I had no experience displaying affection toward Black men.

B. FINDINGS
Within these 54 lecture hours, I realize the possibility exists for
my black skin to blush.

Must control the lips.

II. ANECDOTE

Once, in the produce section, a young white woman asked if the nice-
looking, older Black lady could teach her to make collard greens: how
much water to add to the pot, the spices to sprinkle in and when. Her
Black boyfriend craved greens like those his mother made.

A. ASSESSMENT
Professor: *If he wanted someone to make him collard greens, he
should've been with a Black girl.*

1. RANDOM SURVEY OF BLACKS
It is just the two of us there in the classroom—the color of
our skin the common denominator.

B. DEDUCTION
I was expected to know the difference between a ham hock and
a ham shank.
To be born into the knowledge of how to use them to season
collard greens.

III. ANECDOTE

Forget the patrol car behind us. Relax your shoulders. *You should gun it.
Test them,* I say in jest, my hand in your hair. I am able to make light of
this now, continue, *Thank God it's not the 1950s.*

Tell me why a comment such as this requires me to define miscegenation for you. (Why do I have to define miscegenation for you? Why is there such a long word for this?)

Tell me why I have to explain the importance of this car ride to you:

Because we are not Mildred and Richard Loving.
Because we do not know those old Virginia roads.
Because this is not 1958 when my fingers in your palm
would be ignored as affection and called a felony.

Because the police car that had been trailing us
veered off on another road and left us alone.
Because we can drive to your family's cottage,
I can meet your family this Thanksgiving,
bring pomegranate wine, offer it to the table.

IV. ANECDOTE

It is vegetable stir fry with red asparagus, mashed potatoes with vegan mushroom gravy, pesto tortellini, jellied cranberries, and pumpkin pie: This is what I push around on my plate as your grandfather asks me to help him recall *the word with the "s" sound that the Blacks have a problem saying.*

I know the word, but I won't offer it. As he searches his mind, I say it to myself silently, over and over, wanting to

> *ask* for my nana's collard greens
> *ask* for my mama's candied yams
> *ask* for baked macaroni and cheese
> *ask* for thick slices of cranberry sauce
> *ask* for my father's bourbon pecan pie

Ablation

"After the endometrial ablation procedure, pregnancy is still possible, though unlikely. If you do become pregnant following the procedure, a resulting pregnancy is associated with postoperative complications such as ectopic pregnancy and miscarriage. So, it's important that you use a reliable method of birth control for the remainder of your childbearing years. At 35, you've reached an age where your insurance provider likely won't challenge your choice to have this procedure. Have you made up your mind about having children?"

If the OB/GYN took breaths between these sentences, I didn't hear them.

Have I made up my mind about having children? *Well, clearly. I have.* Since I was a teenager, I've known that I never wanted to bear a child in my body. I've had no desire for anyone to call me "mom." I have written entire poems and blog posts about how I don't want children. I have declared so to parents, siblings, friends, and strangers who asked (and should've known better). Declared most often to a former partner who seemed so determined to convince me to change my mind that I was sure he would sabotage my birth control to impregnate me on purpose.

Have I made up my mind about having children? *Well, damn. Have I?* For a bit too long after I learn that my uterine lining might be cauterized beyond use, I feel more connected to my uterus than I ever thought I would. I don't understand why I care about this, but I do care that some lady wants to steal my uterus.

"I'm 99.9 percent sure I don't want children," I finally say.

The doctor chuckles. She leaves to grab me some literature on the procedure in question.

I survey the room—the stirrups, the ubiquitous anatomical model of the female reproductive system, the rug that is fraying on one edge—and I wonder about all of the women who have been in this room before me.

I think about the women who desperately want children but can't have them. I feel slightly selfish. I feel disappointed in myself for feeling even slightly selfish. I feel so fortunate to have the choice not to have a child. I grieve the erosion of women's reproductive rights that has been happening before my very eyes.

I feel all of this in the 90 seconds or so that the doctor is gone.

The Door Frame

"Didn't you measure the door frame?!" His voice is a shout.

My new neighbors know Matt's voice before they know my voice, my face, my name.

No, I didn't measure the door frame. The couch was the first I had owned that wasn't a loveseat. I have upgraded to a grown-up couch: cream, neutral, does not offend, is pleasant to guests.

No, I didn't measure the door frame. But I *did* know the couch was seventy-one inches long—just long enough for the sixty-nine inches of my body to lie on for naps. It was deep enough to sit cross-legged and read poetry.

No, I didn't measure the door frame. I assumed a standard couch would fit through a standard door frame.

"I can't believe I didn't measure the door frame. I feel so stupid," I cry into his shirt.

It is a gesture my body remembers and doesn't fight. My brain knows that I've given him back his keys, filled out a change of address, will be sleeping alone now, but my body knows no other place to collapse.

The Writing of Fiction

ENG 502: Seminar in the Writing of Fiction
Winter 2012
5 credits

When I was in graduate school, I made a choice that has haunted me ever since.

SCENE: On the first day of class, our professor assigns an in-class writing exercise: ten minutes to write a fiction piece on any subject we wish. We will then take turns reading our pieces aloud. To my right, Matt sits in a chair with a desk attached. At my own desk, I begin to write something very honest, because I know no other way.

When it's my turn to share, I pick up my notebook and read:

"Come on, let's have a baby. Just one. Our baby would be beautiful," he says to me all too casually as he holds his rocks glass. The words "our baby" reverberate in my ears, and I miss the rest of his words. Then I begin to imagine our baby...

She is 19 years old, tickling her throat to empty herself of dinner.

She is 14 years old, fending off the violence of 14-year-old boys.

She is 12 years old, grazing blades over her skin in her bedroom.

She is 10 years old, ogled by men older than her father.

She is a plus sign on a pregnancy test.

And I am her mama, all because I said "yes" after one too many whiskey cokes.

I put down my notebook. I don't look in Matt's direction for several moments after. I know, and he knows; the autobiography in this fiction is clear. I even borrowed his exact words *Come on, let's have a baby. Just one. Our baby would be beautiful.*

In this moment, I have hinted, finally, that I don't want his child.

I am no longer fluent in the language of "should," but if I were, I imagine that I should feel bad about this act. I don't. What haunts me is not the brazen act or my avoidance of eye contact or the way I possibly shattered his heart in front of ten classmates and our professor.

In short, here is what happens once the piece becomes more than scribbles in a notebook:

A woman meets a man who is just a few years younger than she. He is the cashier at the grocery store where she is a frequent buyer of cabernet blends and cupcakes with sprinkles. They meet, they fall, they move in, he fucks up. He wants a baby, and she doesn't. He tells her what he wants after a few whiskey cokes. She doesn't tell him what she doesn't want, and instead says something vague enough to not lose him. He wants the baby to have her eyes, her skin color. Then, they are newlyweds. He wants a baby, and she doesn't. One night, he wipes her chin while she is crumpled on their bathroom floor after an eating disorder relapse. She decides that this quality—amongst other everyday things—means that she should probably have his baby. So she does. Their baby arrives, a girl who is just a bit too small to take home just yet. Baby girl has his eyes. Amongst all of the congratulations, only one person quietly asks, "Are you happy?"

The end.

I created fictional backgrounds for our characters, but other than a few mentions of how ambivalent my fictional counterpart was, I gave him *exactly* what he wanted. I gave him his story in fiction because I knew, otherwise, I wouldn't give him what he wanted.

These many years later, I want to revise the story. I want to go back. I want to submit a different manuscript. I want to not be an archetype of a wife and mother who gives a man exactly what he wants.

Even in fiction.

COURSE GRADE: A

Slam

ENG 457: Special Topics in Poetry Writing
Slam & Spoken Word
Winter 2012
5 Credits

Poetry Slam Rules

1. The Golden Rule of Poetry Slam: The points are not the point. The point is poetry.
2. Each poem must be the original work of the poet.
3. Each poet is allotted three minutes to perform one poem. There is a 10-second grace period, after which the poet will incur time penalties.
4. Just the poet and their poem on stage. No props, costumes, or musical accompaniment are allowed.
5. Five audience members are selected on a volunteer basis to serve as judges. The judges consider the quality of the writing and performance of each poem and assign a score on a scale from 0.0 to 10. For every score, the highest and lowest scores are dropped, and the final score for the round is calculated by adding the three remaining scores together.

* * *

Just the poet and their poem on stage.

In a place that is equal parts art gallery, café, wine bar, and event venue, Matt sits in the audience amongst dozens of others.

From the stage, I choose to tell him (and a room full of strangers) that I will not take his last name if we marry. I look at his face as I perform my poem "Will You Take This, Woman?". I look at his face as I deliver all 661 words within less than three minutes.

I tell him I do want to marry him, but he must understand that I cannot take his last name. From birth, I've been defined by my relationship to men. I tell him how schoolteachers would use my father's last name to scold Miss Smith for talking, Miss Smith for passing notes. "Miss Smith" was always used for silence. Would being his Mrs. be any different?

I tell him that, thereafter, I vowed no man would ever mark me or possess me again. I would prefer to shed my last name and simply be Danielle. Alas, even then...

When my mother was pregnant with me, 24 years old, ultrasound gel covering swollen belly, the doctor told her to prepare room for her beautiful baby boy. She set her hands to looking through scripture, fingers finally landing on the book of Daniel, meaning "God is my judge." Daniel, a prophet who speaks in visions and dreams. Maybe she thought—like his namesake—her son too could face any lion's den and be found faultless in the eyes of God.

I tell him to note my two extra letters: the "L" and the "E." Daniel is an abbreviation of me. I am "Danielle." I am more expansive than Daniel.

In my final words, I tell him:

Let me become like a map that you cannot refold:
let me remain open and stubborn and take up space
I will not be quiet and diminutive
I will be loud and unruly
Let my name not equal me, and not even be forever
unchanged, but for now, let my name remain

I step off stage, walk to the table where he sits, kiss him on the head, and take my seat next to him.

On her way out the door, a woman grabs me lightly by the arm, pulls me in like she's telling me a secret: "I didn't take my husband's last name when I got married." She winks and walks out.

Maybe not the most tactful way to tell him. But the only way I know. Perhaps here, with witnesses, he cannot pretend he has not heard me.

* * *

POETRY SLAM: 2nd PLACE

COURSE GRADE: A

The Rules

1. Every time you wash your hands, you must wash your hands three times
2. You must wash your hands before touching these surfaces (see Rule 1)
3. Any items that enter the bedroom must remain there, as they are contaminated
4. You cannot wear any clothing in bed*
5. If you enter the bedroom, you must stay there or immediately take a shower after leaving, as you are contaminated
6. Do not touch coins, as they are contaminated
7. You must wear gloves if you touch items beneath the kitchen sink, as they are contaminated

When Matt's not home, I don't follow his rules. Sometimes, I run my unwashed hands across the spines of the books in his bookcase—his most sacred space. It feels defiant. Like I'm getting away with something.

No. I'm not being controlled. Not me.
I would know if I were. I did the research. I'm a feminist.
It's not his fault.

*"Ok, fine. You can wear bottoms during that time of the month but no other time."

Black, Radical Feminist

What Matt loves most about me, he says, is that I am a Black, radical feminist.

Black? Yes. Feminist? Yes. But radical? There is nothing radical, really, about me or my feminism. Except, I suppose, being Black and a feminist in a white supremacist, patriarchal society like ours is radical.

Still, every time I express an opinion or behave in a manner true to my "Black, radical feminist" self, he does not like it, let alone love it.

When I open my mouth to object as grandfather condemns sex workers—only the workers, not the men employing their services—Matt squeezes my clenched fist beneath the table, glares at me, and shakes his head to quiet me.

When I inform him I do not wish to have children, he tries to convince me otherwise. "Let's just have one," he says, "Our baby would be beautiful." He wants our child to have the caramel-colored skin that this Black woman and this white man would create.

When I tell him I will not change my last name if we should marry, he is disappointed. "It's just not normal," he says.

The man I'm dating is white, blue eyed, and from a small city in the Midwest with a Black population of 2 percent.

What he loves about dating a "Black, radical feminist," I realize, is what he believes his proximity to me says about himself: *Look how radical* I *am.*

A Woman's Study

"You do realize that you just described emotional abuse, like, exactly...right?" my friend asks into the phone, her voice just above a whisper.

How jarring this must be for her. We hadn't talked for a while. The last time we spoke, I told her how Matt and I had started dating.

I had gushed to her about how our first date that wasn't a date started on moving day. We had only known each other a couple of weeks when he offered to help me move from my apartment after overhearing me recounting my roommate horror story. After returning the moving truck, I treated him to breakfast at a café downtown and then drove him home. I wanted to return to my new apartment and line my kitchen shelves with shelf paper. He convinced me otherwise. We went to the independent movie theater downtown and watched a movie. After the movie, I wanted to return to my new apartment and unpack. He convinced me otherwise. The evening culminated with us at a café, talking love and friendship over hot chocolate: *Is romantic love a wholly different type of affection than friendship or just a higher level of friendship?*

I had shared with her that, after we'd been dating for one month, he'd already asked me to move in. Shortly after, we began looking at elopement packages at bed and breakfasts.

That was then.

Now, a series of "But it's not his fault" statements and how he tells me that he will have nothing left to live for if I leave him.

* * *

He controls every decision of our lives from what I wear to bed, how many times I wash my hands, what shows and movies we stream, the temperature of our apartment (he always runs hot, I'm always cold. So, the compromise: he blasts the air conditioning while I curl up under a blanket or freeze). He objects when I want to drive my own car and has changed all my radio presets to his favorite stations. I sit in the passenger seat of the car I pay for and stare out the window, singing songs to myself.

I stay quiet because I don't like conflict. Instead, I research on the internet "How to live with someone who has OCD." Through research, I learn strategies to support him. I also learn how trauma presents itself in *so* many ways. (It's not his fault).

It's easier to just keep my feelings to myself. I don't want to impact his mental health any further. Don't want to stigmatize him.

* * *

"You do realize that you just described emotional abuse, like, exactly…right?"
I think back to myself just a handful of years ago.

WOM STD M108S: Violence Against Women
FALL 2004
4 Credits

I had done the research. Known what signs to look for. Read about the cumulative effect of a person being completely dominated without their awareness. I had written 6,000 words.

Danielle Smith
Violence Against Women
2 December 2004

"But I Love Him": Emotional Abuse in Adolescent Intimate Relationships

Defined it. Cited the statistics. Explored how abuse intensifies over time, presents in different forms. How violent behavior is learned. How socially constructed gender role norms correlate with perpetration and victimization.

Described the stages that make up the complex cycle of abuse. How verbal and emotional violence are almost always precursors to physical violence. How abuse manifests.

How abuse systematically erodes one's self-confidence, sense of self-worth, self-concept, and ability to trust in our own perceptions.

How growing up in a household or culture of violence without any examples of healthy relationships can lead to a person becoming a victim and/or perpetrator of abuse.

It's normalized behavior, so it's hard to detect.

COURSE GRADE: A-

* * *

So, I stayed. I stayed because I said his behavior wasn't his fault. Instead, I made it my fault and my problem and my responsibility.

And then it became my undoing.

When my mother left my father, she had a convoy of people help: her children, her mom, her brother, his wife.

When I left, it was just in the way that he and I started: simply me, him, and a moving truck. Is that symmetry?

It is a gesture that made me wonder—for longer than I should have —if I was wrong to leave.

He is a man who will help you move your bed frame, your boxes, your new couch—even as you're moving them away from him.

References

I would observe Matt as he cycled through his rituals. Who was he before life happened to him?

Someone needs to take care of him. If I don't stay with him, who will? If I don't love him, who will? Someone needs to love him.

I decided that someone was me.

I asked myself, "Could I do this? Could I *really* do this? Could I set aside my own desires, comfort, and well-being? Could I deny the possibility of a relationship with someone else whom I would love to take care of a man whom I do not love? Remain in a relationship that makes me feel as though I am suffocating? Could I really do this for the rest of my life?"

I decided that I could. It probably wouldn't be too bad.

It probably wouldn't be too bad...

It probably wouldn't be too bad?!

In that moment, I knew that it was time to get the hell out. Because I really *could* have stayed with him for the rest of my life—my own self be damned.

* * *

"Why do you make others infants in their relationship to you?" my therapist asks.

Ouch.

Everything in me wants to fight back and say, "I call 'bullshit.' I think your assessment of me is a little unfair. What about...? Have you considered...?" I feel the challenge in me rise then quiet.

In my silence, I remember that I like her. A lot. Mostly because she does not mince words. I remind myself that I have sought a therapist because every single committed or commitment-adjacent relationship with a man I've had has had the same pattern. The common denominator is me.

In her silence, her eyes issue a challenge.

The last time someone looked at me this way was when I, for the hundredth time, was complaining about my relationship. Drew had listened calmly as I recounted Matt's most recent transgressions. When I finally took a breath, he said, "It's because you don't love him." I blinked at Drew, thinking of a retort.

If I don't stay with him, who will? If I don't love him, who will?

I, apparently, do not think very highly of this person with whom I am in a relationship. How could I? I have predicted that no one in this *entire* world—of all the people he may encounter in his lifetime—would ever want to be in a relationship with or could love him. Too much life had happened to him. He was too broken. Too flawed. In my assessment of him, I have deemed him unworthy of love.

I had told myself that I must leave my relationship lest I be consumed whole. What I realize now is this: I must leave for both our sakes.

We both deserved better.

* * *

I learn that there is language for behaviors that are part of my "normal."

Codependency. C-O-D-E-P-E-N-D-E-N-C-Y. Codependency.

I have to ask several times before it (somewhat) begins to make sense.

"So, *how exactly* does my being compassionate toward people make me codependent?"

I jot down notes as my therapist talks.

Later, I head to the internet and look up the term. Apparently, there's a whole organization with meetings and support groups for my "normal."

I read the list of patterns and characteristics that can help answer the question "Am I codependent?" With its headings and subheadings, the page almost looks like a job posting outlining the required and preferred qualifications for their ideal candidate.

Well, damn. If I were applying for this position, I would be well qualified.

- Excellent at multi-tasking: Can simultaneously feel responsible for solving other people's problems—even if they did not ask for help—and feel drained and resentful due to helping them.
- Wonderful attention to detail: Sensitive to the energies and emotions of others to the point of crushing overwhelm.
- Advanced skill in teambuilding and collaboration: Committed to compromising own needs and wants to avoid rejection and confrontation with others.

References available upon request.

On Consoling Men Who Cry

I

When my mother finally left you, she sought space
to unfold, to exhale her held breath—to unbecome
the mother of four who had collapsed into her own body
because she'd had nowhere else to go
She was 50 years old

Even though I had asked for this since before
I even knew the weight of the word "leave"
Even though I knew many of the reasons she finally left you
(because I had kept a running list myself)
Even though I used the phrase *Why don't you just leave him?*
so many times it began to feel more familiar
in my mouth than my own first name
I said *yes* when you called. Asked me to move in with you
Help you with the mortgage

Dad, you were how I learned to say *yes* to men
who would be practiced in damaging me
But I don't blame you

II

Here is how you remember your own father: gone
With his passing, a different absence

Dad, here is how I remember you:
The tower of your body,
the great boom of your voice
Your face a malleable square
of facial expressions:
turbulence, rage, fatigue

After Mom was gone:
You, a crumbling edifice
Your face learned grief, regret,
how to be damp with tear water
But I don't blame you

III

How I was taught papier-mâché:

Step one: Blow up a balloon
Step two: Wet strips of newspaper in liquid starch
Step three: Cover balloon until it no longer is visible
Step four: Allow to dry completely
Step five: Destroy the balloon inside so that all that remains is shell

I always felt sad for the balloon
I'd wonder: Did the balloon know it would be used
    for this purpose?
I'd wonder: For what else could this balloon have been used?

I do not recall what age I was when I noticed my mother
began to become the balloon

IV

Woman (noun): a vessel; a receptacle
Love (verb): to render oneself empty for

V

When this man
     whom I met in September at a wine bar on Holly Street
     whom I hope someday will let me call him Husband
     who calls me My Dear and looks at me across candlelight
     whom I've given the power to manipulate my self-esteem simply
     with how frequently he may or may not dial my phone number

When he
     is sitting across from me, telling me a story so devastating
     that I can almost feel the room collapse under its weight

When he
     despite his best efforts, has been betrayed,
     yes, by the water gathering at his eyelids,
     but more so by the muscles in his face
     (and he has tried hard not to break; I can see it)

I think: *Go ahead. This is my inheritance*
What I am told I am for. What I was made *to do*
I don't know why I want to touch the pads of my fingers
to his forearm, hold his hand, but I do

I can intellectualize this right now and wonder
if I am using his pain to have a reason to touch him

I could berate myself for being an opportunist—
for using this as a way to hold his hand for the first time
But I won't go there today

So I will just sit with my skin on his skin and wonder
if he can feel it, *them:*
The men who came before him—first you, Dad
Then the Point Guard, The Ranger, The Philosopher
The men I have loved

VI

Here is what I've noticed in the faces of men who cry:
They cry just as they've been conditioned to live—fight

I see it in you, Dad: the tremulous dance of your facial muscles
(and I wish I knew what muscles they are,
understood the physiology of what is happening
to your face right now, but I don't. I want so much to
be poetic about this moment, but I can't,
because I don't even know the muscles' names)

I see it in you: you are fighting for control
You don't want to be softened,
to be threatened by this betrayal
of whom you have been told to be,
especially in front of me—a woman now,
but still your youngest daughter
~~for~~ whom you have ~~been~~ taught
to be strong, to protect
But I need you to be soft. Show me
Let me see that we are the same inside
We both contain muscles whose names we may never learn

VII

The first time you came to Bellingham, I took you
to Boulevard Park to show you the water
Maybe I told you, maybe I didn't tell you
that it is my favorite place
I sit on a bench to be present with the water
even though I fear it. The water is a reminder
to breathe, that there is still cause
to keep breathing

I sit and watch the sunsets. The sunsets there linger
with such brilliance that I will risk my own eyesight
just to keep them in my gaze
Looking at you now requires my eyes to recall that boldness
I can see that you are sinking beneath something
What horizon is taking you?

VIII

I want so much to name those muscles in your face
I want to be able to console you in the way you need
I want to know the right thing to do, to say
But I am just as helpless as you are, just as powerless
against this *thing*, this word, this verb we call "cry"

I don't blame either one of us
You were taught not to be this vulnerable, and I—
I am supposed to know how to tap into what I am told
is my innate ability to nurture
I guess we both failed today

So I will give you my four fingers pressed to your forearm,
and you can read them however you need

7 things

...that probably contributed to my outing myself as a feminist during Thanksgiving "What are you thankful for?" circle, 1998

CW: Violence, sexualized violence

1. That we learn to anticipate it. In third grade, the boys declared "Friday Flip-up Days," so we girls didn't wear dresses or skirts those days. Or those of us who were bold enough to still wear dresses wore shorts beneath them. We had not learned to use our collective voices to tell someone what was happening to us. We did learn to whisper "Remember tomorrow is Friday..." in each other's ears. How intricately we adjust to our own victimization.

2. How often I asked my mother, "Why don't you just leave him?" and offered her reasons to leave as if she didn't already have her list memorized. Me in my 9-year-old precociousness: "Why don't you just leave him?" My 11-year-old impudence: "Why don't you just leave him?" My 14-year-old rebelliousness: "Why don't you just leave him?"

3. The sixth-grade boy I reported for sexual harassment, as soon as I learned the language. The presenter didn't know she had offered me a

path out of silence, given me a compact way to explain how he had violated me and my body. The sixth-grade boy felt betrayed and asked, "Why would you report me? Why would you do this to me?"

4. Though my mouth said, "Because it's true! And that's what you were doing!" Though my brain said, "I was justified!" I felt guilty.

5. That I challenged my mother's responses to my question: "Why don't you just leave him?" That I told her she needed to leave as if she didn't already know. As if, at 9, 11, or 14 years old, I knew a *damn* thing more than she.

6. When a 14-year-old boy who wore malice like a uniform snatched me from a dark hallway, pushed me down on a bed, had the entire length of his body pressed into mine, his weight expelling the air from my lungs, his right hand around my neck, my parents and his in the next room, I thought: *Don't scream. You will get him in trouble.*

7. As I was audience to the chapters of my parents' marriage story, I read my mother's staying as cowardice, her tactical, silent strength as weakness. I saw a weathered shack in need of protection from the tempest. I didn't see that she was a castle on a hill. Her very spine made of stone.

Rough Draft

"7 things..." is a version of the piece I referenced in my TEDx Talk. The piece I read at an open mic that motivated a woman to walk up to me with tears in her eyes and say, "We need more strong female voices like yours. Thank you."

Imagine. I almost didn't read "7 things..." that night. It had only recently come to life. A half hour or so before I left for the open mic, I was struck with the idea, so I wrote it on the back of another piece that I *had* planned to read. As such, "7 things..." was rough, and I hadn't had time to practice, but I felt it was important to share.

I'm not sure what content the audience expected to hear after I read the title in full: "7 things that probably contributed to my outing myself as a feminist during Thanksgiving 'What are you thankful for?' circle, 1998." Whatever they expected probably wasn't what came next.

When I read the name of the piece aloud, several members of the crowd laughed. I can't really blame them. They didn't know that— between the long title and the first sentence—the tone would shift radically.

Are we ever prepared for the experiences that happen to us?

Processing...

Instead of swinging and thrashing and screaming, I decided to use my learned skills to try to convince the teenage boy that removing his hand from my throat would be in his best interest.

Within seconds of him pressing his hand to my throat, my mind accessed its lessons and began a sequence:

1. With your eyes, implore *Please stop*.
2. Remember: Your voice is not for this. Your voice is not for objection.
3. Whisper "Please stop" so our parents in the other room do not hear.
4. Remember: You must have integrity. You do not get others in trouble.
5. *You* will get in trouble for somehow tempting him with your body.

I imagined the aftermath of what would happen if I managed to scream: My father rushing into the room, grabbing the boy from atop my body, and...I don't know what would happen next, but I have seen my father react to lesser evils, so I will leave this at *imagine*.

Would the boy's father at first stand in the hallway looking on, wondering what happened? Would he then, upon finally understanding, try to push himself into the room in an intuitive desire to protect his own child? The boy's father and my father were good friends. Would their friendship be ruined? So. No scream.

I marvel at my mind sometimes. Fascinating what processes can run through a girl's mind in less than two minutes.

Aftermath

CW: Violence

About a decade ago, a male Facebook friend wrote a post describing a situation he had encountered that day. While in a store, he saw that a female customer had dropped an item on the floor. After the woman started walking away, he picked up the item and followed her to give the item back. He had called out to her to get her attention, but the woman ignored his calls and hurried along to the checkout. He arrived at the checkout shortly after her and handed the item to the cashier, noting, "Here, this belongs to her, because *she** was too good to turn around when I tried to give it back to her."

In reactions to the post, the consensus was that the woman was a bitch who assumed he was trying to come on to her.

I read the post and the comments. I considered my own myriad experiences.

Thought about how no situation I've ever been in that involved a boy or man following me has ever had a positive result. Like when I was walking from the bathroom then was snatched out of a hallway and thrown onto a bed—not once, but twice. Different hallways, different people, but a nearly identical experience roughly a decade apart.

**He was careful to point out that, at this moment, he had made a dramatic show of giving her a contemptuous head toss.*

Thought about how I feel that I live most of my life in a state of perpetual aftermath.

While I normally shy away from potential conflict (especially on the internet), I felt called to try to surface the humanity of the woman who was being publicly condemned. I commented that there was no way of knowing this woman's experience and to not automatically assume she was a bitch. I offered that it was possible the woman may have had past experiences with violence that made her respond in that way.

Unanimously, the commenters judged my comment as ludicrous.

Shortly after I posted my comment, a female commenter posted, "I get tired of women sometimes. Like, sometimes women just need to shut up, get on their knees, and open their mouths."

Not surprisingly, her post received an enthusiastic series of "likes" from men, and, disappointingly, a number of "likes" from other women.

Lesson: As a woman, do not use your mouth to speak. Solely use your mouth to provide sexual pleasure to men.

Plan: Reject.

Request

CW: Sexualized violence

The final report for the formal complaint is dated January 26, 2012, just one day before my 28th birthday. Happy Birthday, me.

The package arrives in a very official-looking clasp envelope. I will not read this report right now, I decide. I will read it when I'm ready. I have no definition for what I mean by "ready." All I know: not now.

I will, instead, for years, move the clasp envelope from one stack of documents to another until I finally move it to a box labeled "To File."

Five years later, after the report and its box have moved with me to three different apartments, I decide I am ready (still no definition). I open the envelope.

Within the first five pages, the report reminds me that on December 2, 2011, a staff member in the investigating office ("Investigator") interviewed Ms. Smith ("Complainant"), and Complainant had provided a written statement.

Within the first five pages, the report reminds me that the Complainant wrote a colleague ("Respondent") an email to address his behavior.

What the report does not state is that, when the Complainant wrote the email, she had two main aims:

1. Be direct and clear that she wanted the behavior to stop
2. Have documentation so she would have proof that she said "stop"

The second paragraph of page five of the report reads: "Ms. Smith's email indicates that she did not find the complained-of actions offensive until around the time she sent that email."

What the hell? Where did they get that from?!

I flip through the pages to the attached document that the staff had graciously marked with "Tab A" on a yellow page flag. After flipping past the page that contained a list of the Respondent's behaviors, I find my email. I skim the email, looking for evidence, poised and ready to defend the Complainant. I practically am drafting my letter of dissent in my head.

"God, Danielle, really?!" *The Complainant served him a feedback sandwich?*

In pedagogical training, we were taught the "feedback sandwich" technique to provide feedback to students in our writing classes. The technique is as follows: you begin with positive feedback, follow with your critique, then end with more positive feedback. What you authentically want to say is sandwiched between (sometimes inauthentic) positive affirmation. The goal of the feedback sandwich is to provide critical feedback in a positive and encouraging manner, so students won't disengage from the learning process. Even if a draft was the worst draft in the history of drafts, you were *strongly* encouraged to find something positive to highlight in your feedback. The problem with students, though, is that they're smart. They know this technique. And they call bullshit.

From: Complainant
To: Respondent
Date: Sun, 27 Mar 2011
Subject: Request

Begin with a positive: The Complainant sets the context for this message by informing the Respondent that she had learned of some false statements the Respondent had made claiming that they had a sexual relationship. The Complainant wrote, before this recent development, "I have never taken your behaviors seriously or offensively." She says that he has been a "fun and interesting person to be around." [While the Respondent had indeed behaved inappropriately toward the Complainant in the time they had known each other—making sexually coded gestures, comments, and looks—the Respondent displayed this behavior to practically everyone, irrespective of gender. The Complainant disregarded the Respondent's conduct, as did their colleagues, mainly because the Respondent seemed like nothing more than a provocateur; he enjoyed flouting societal mores.]

Layer in the criticism: The Complainant does not appreciate being the subject of the Respondent's falsehoods. She requests that he stop with the comments, the looks, the gestures. Keep her name out of his mouth.

End with a positive: The Complainant would like to be civil because their department is small, and they have to work together.

If I were to serve the Complainant a feedback sandwich for her email, I might say something like this:

This is a solid first attempt to assert yourself, and I see your intention coming through. To better align with your intended goals for this email, you might consider simply stating that the behavior was inappropriate and that you want the behavior to stop. Overall, I admire your attention to detail in setting the boundaries.

But my unbuffered feedback?

Omit the bullshit.

While I respect the Complainant for sending the email at all, she was so...*polite*. Her language so tentative: "I would like you to refrain from....," "I would appreciate if you would please stop...."
The subject line was "Request," not "Demand" or "Command."
The Complainant was essentially asking his permission.

Reading this damning email was excellent preparation for the written statement.

I had wasted no time. In the first paragraph of my statement, I had written, "Not reporting him is a failure on my part, and I should have done so before now." The paragraph concludes with my taking responsibility that the situation worsened and acknowledging that my inaction may have caused others to have had experiences like mine. I devoted nearly as much space to blaming myself as I did to detailing his history of inappropriate comments, looks, gestures, and physical contact.

This paragraph and the statement housing it almost didn't exist at all. But, on a Friday in December, I was working in my office when a colleague walked in. She asked if I was going to submit a complaint. I waffled, said several noncommittal statements, avoided eye contact.

And then. She told me that several women in the department who had agreed to file a complaint had, one by one, chosen not to—for undisclosed reasons. She pleaded with me to submit my complaint.

"I'm beginning to feel like a pariah," she said.

I submitted my complaint that same day. While I was okay letting myself down, I would be damned if I let her go through that alone.

So, I wrote.

On December 2, 2011, I wrote about behaviors that hadn't bothered me much before but should have. As I wrote, what became evident to me was that I had, over my lifetime, become too accustomed to accepting a litany of unacceptable behaviors. And, at times, making excuses for them.

As I wrote, I did not consider how, in my email dated March 27, 2011, I had used language in a very particular way. I had carefully chosen my language to avoid making him too uncomfortable. The first draft was direct, but I felt it was *too* direct; I didn't want to make him feel bad. So I revised it. Added some positive statements. Softened the language. Hit "Send."

And in trying to limit his discomfort, I discredited myself.

No "he said, she said." Not "his word against hers."

Just my own words used against me.

Catalogue

In the years since the open mic, I've returned to "7 things..." again and again with new eyes. The details get a bit finer, though the stories are the same. Each time, the wisdom and perspective I bring with me make me experience the piece differently.

I originally referred to "7 things..." as a poem because I had no other succinct word for it. Really, it's a catalogue. Some "things" are not on the list—either because I didn't think of them at the moment or because they happened to me later.

* * *

8. Upon arrival at our church in LA, elder women stand at the doors handing out pieces of cloth. In no time at all, I notice they're only giving the cloth to the women and girls. I'm a girl, so the elder hands me a cloth. I ask my mother, "What's this cloth for?" She tells me it's a lap scarf. Females place it over their laps when they wear a skirt or dress. They cover their laps so the pastor isn't tempted. *Why do I need to cover myself? Can the pastor not control his eyes? It would be* my *fault the pastor was tempted?*

9. Every day, I walk home from middle school and a classmate follows me home trying to touch the parts of my body my mother told me never to let someone touch. My friends begin to detour from their

own routes home to walk partway home with me so I won't be alone with him and his hands.

10. I am perhaps 14 years old and walking out of a grocery store with my mother. As I pass, a man as old as my grandfather tells me in no uncertain terms that he likes what he sees and wants to see more. My mother whisks me away, telling him I am too young for him to talk to me that way.

11. My senior year in college, I am standing in line at a Starbucks in West LA waiting for my latte. The man next to me begins polite small talk. I polite small talk back. When the barista calls my name, I grab my drink and head toward the exit. As I walk toward the door, the man quickly picks up his coffee cup and newspaper and gets up from the table. *Shit!* I know what happens next; I've lived this before.

The man follows me outside into the dark parking lot. I walk with my coffee cup in one hand. In the other, I hold my car keys with the ignition key wedged between my fingers the way the self-defense training instructs you to hold your keys in case you need to use them to defend yourself. I consider my options if this escalates: Can I quickly get into my car without him forcing me inside? Would I be faster than him if I ran back into the store to seek help? *Why didn't I just go back into the store when I saw him begin to follow me? I'm so stupid!*

I finally reach my car, leaving room to run away if I need to. I put my coffee cup on the roof of my car so my left hand is available to fight, if necessary. Hoping he'll leave, I say, "Have a good night." My experiences have taught me to say this in the most neutral way possible. *Don't be too dismissive, or he'll get angry.*

He asks if he can call me, take me out sometime. I decline. But he is a King in an unspecified land; I could be his Queen. I say I'm not interested. He disagrees. I tell him to leave me alone. He does not. I say that if he doesn't leave me alone, I will call security. Why? "Because you're scaring me." How? "You followed me to my car in the middle of the night and have refused to leave when I repeatedly asked you to!" Finally, he's decided he's had enough and storms away, flapping his arms, the pages of the newspaper blowing in the wind.

"You're a lesbian! Why do you have to be a lesbian?!"

12. I am 21 years old, freshly graduated from college, and am working at a temp job to gain some marketable skills. On my first day at the job, Cliff, the guy who works in the warehouse, asks if I'd like to talk and get to know each other on a lunch break. I agree, and we walk to a local sandwich shop. At the restaurant, Cliff notices my tongue piercing and asks if I have any others. I feel the question is a bit personal, but I reply that I have a navel piercing. He asks, "Will you show it to me?" I decline. He persists, and I say *no* for (what I assumed would be) the final time. For several days after, when I need to deliver items to the warehouse, Cliff asks me to show him my navel piercing. I look fit, he says. I look like I would have a nice stomach. Can he see my abs? After nearly a week of these comments, I speak to the supervisor and report Cliff's behavior. That afternoon, Cliff confronts me: "Why would you report me?" I request a new job assignment.

13. Given my age and life experiences, I should know better than to use words like "should." Still, when filing the report, I say, "I know how he can be. I shouldn't have offered to drive him home, but he was drunk, and I worried about his safety. I shouldn't have gone inside his apartment. I shouldn't have had more to drink." My voice a refrain of "I shouldn't have... I shouldn't have..." Between the Investigator and myself, I'm not sure who is more disappointed in me.

x. There are so many other things.

Cause & Effect

The stories come from all over. We overhear conversations. We read the articles. We scroll through social media feeds:

"What did she expect? She shouldn't have gone into his room. She knew what he wanted."

"Well, when you dress like that, you shouldn't be surprised when something happens. She was putting it out there."

"She was asking for it."

* * *

Quiz

A group of 10-year-old female pep squad members and their adult female squad leader are walking along the street from the local middle school back to their elementary school. A car carrying three adult men pulls up next to the group and drives slowly alongside them. The adult men on the passenger side of the vehicle hang out of the windows and proceed to leer at, whistle at, and make sexualized comments to the 10-year-old girls.

What was the cause of this situation?

SELECT ONE:

A. The 10-year-old girls were wearing skirts
B. The 10-year-old girls were wearing t-shirts
C. The 10-year-old girls were holding pom poms
D. The 10-year-old girls called attention to themselves with their chatter and lively movements
E. The 10-year-old girls should have changed into more modest clothing before walking down this street
F. All of the above

The narrative about sexualized violence that our society provides to us would lead us to believe there are no other options for this scenario. After all, we girls must have done *something* wrong. What business do little girls have walking so brazenly down the street?

Asking for It

What was I doing when I was "asking for it"?

I was playing on a playground
I was sitting in my classroom
I was walking down a hallway
I was walking home from school
I was walking out of a grocery store
I was walking to my car
I was working at a temp job
I was walking down a (different) hallway
I was walking to school

Playing. Sitting. Walking. Working.

What "asking" is: The present participle of the verb "to ask."
What "asking" is not: What I was doing.

Stop

I wonder what goes through their minds when we finally confront or report them. What intricate mental processes do they initiate?

"Well, Danielle, you didn't *exactly* tell me that what I was doing bothered you. You didn't say no. So...can you *really* blame me for my behavior?"

I really want to. I will ask you, instead, to question your lessons.

What or who trained you to follow a 12-year-old girl every day trying to touch her body as you're both walking home from school?

What messaging did you receive that you felt it would be appropriate to ask a coworker to lift her shirt to show you a part of her body? What or who authorized you to feel entitled to view her body despite her repeated protests?

What or who taught you to grab a girl as she's walking down a hallway from the bathroom, throw her on a bed, and begin to choke her?

Listen.

I sometimes said no with my mouth, but I *always* said no with my body. I said no by running from your hands. I said no by backing away. I said no by swatting your hands away from my flesh. I said no with my grip on your forearm and terror in my eyes. I said no by not saying yes.

You say I didn't put a stop to it.

Why did you put a *start* to it?

I am always held accountable for my silence.

At what point are you held accountable for your behavior?

Frequently Asked Questions (FAQs)

But what about when we *do* say no?

Q: But what *type* of no is it?
A: No.

Q: Is it a no that actually means "yes"?
A: No.

Q: Is it a no with an open invitation to try again?
A: No.

Q: Is it a no with an asterisk?
A: No.

Q: Is it a no with a comma?
A: No.

Q: Is it a no with an ellipsis?
A: No.

A: It's a no.
A: Complete sentence.
A: Full stop.
A: .

Stories

The curriculum in my lessons about boys and men

Males are sexual creatures who lust with their eyes and are unable to control their desires. Once males are sexually excited, that urge needs to be fulfilled *somehow*. Never let a boy or man give or buy you anything because he'll expect something (i.e., sex) in return. Boys and "real" men do not cry. Men's egos are fragile, and they are easily emasculated. "Real" men do not ask for directions, read instructions, or say the words "I don't know." Men are "simple" and would be utterly helpless without women. The man is the head of the home and is deserving of my respect and deference. If a man isn't allowed to assume his rightful place as a leader, then he will experience role confusion. Though the man may not actually be in control, you must make him believe he is. Only men should hold positions in office because they are natural leaders. Meeting the "right" man will change my mind about not wanting to have children. Men don't respect women anymore because of the feminists.

Some of these stories were passed down to me like an inheritance. Others were taught to me by boys and men as performance art.

I want a different story.

* * *

The curriculum in my lessons about girls and women

The first woman, Eve, was a biblical delinquent who caused the fall of man. Females cannot be smart *and* attractive. Females cannot interact with each other without being catty, passive-aggressive, and competitive. Women cannot be effective leaders because they're too emotional. Working in an office full of women is the precise recipe for drama and trouble, and *definitely* never work for a female supervisor. We cannot trust a woman's judgment. Women deserve to be paid less because they really should be in the home, anyway; they're taking jobs from men. Women invent stories of sexual assault because they regret their previous behavior and have since changed their minds. Women invent stories of sexual assault because they are trying to advance professionally and/or profit financially. Women invent stories of sexual assault because they seek to destroy the lives and careers of men because they disagree with their politics. Feminism has corrupted women's minds, ruined happy marriages, and emasculated men.

Most of the storytellers were women themselves.

I want a different story.

* * *

I have hope for a future in which women's rights are not human rights marked with an asterisk.

I have hope for a future in which gender has no bearing on the recognition or celebration of our humanity.

I have hope for a future in which we all learn, live, and tell better stories than this.

Full stop.

IV

A Woman's Work

Disembodied

"Where do you feel that in your body? What is your body telling you right now?" my therapist asks.

My body?

I don't know what my body is saying.

To move us along in the session, I create a story when asked to reflect on my mindfulness body scan.

"I feel tightness in my chest," my voice a question mark masquerading as a period.

What does she expect me to say?

I speak *to* my body; it doesn't speak back.

Hunger

When do I stop being hungry?

I wondered how anorexics I had read about were able to control their hunger for so long. I thought there must be a hunger switch that turned off or some magical point when you stopped being hungry and could live with no or very few calories. I thought I was doing anorexia wrong.

When do I stop being hungry?

The girls in the internet forums seemed to be in a state of utter control. They would brag about how many days had passed without food, their tactics to hide that they weren't eating, shared secrets for how to *look* as though they'd eaten. The ones who did eat would share strategies for how they tricked their body into believing it was nourished. Stories upon stories of those who knelt in front of toilets or bathtubs or stood at sinks or wherever else they could empty themselves and called this practice "control."

I wanted to be in control like them, but I felt like a failure because I couldn't tolerate starving. Reluctantly, I began to allow small amounts of food. When I was on the volleyball team my sophomore year, I chose to eat only as much as I needed so I wouldn't feel dizzy. My daily calorie intake ranged 200–800 calories; on average, I ate 400 calories a day.

I ate solely to quiet the evidence of my hunger. *Are you happy? I gave you food. I gave you what you wanted.* After eating, I knew there was a brief window of time before digestion during which I could rid my body of the food and not risk gaining weight. I had created a system so I could satisfy my body's hunger without having to deal with the consequences.

Or so I thought.

Having practiced a cycle of food restriction and purging since 14 years old, I had become masterful at inducing vomiting.

However, one time in particular was different. My tried-and-true method didn't work. I tried and tried but nothing came. I tried while tears poured down my cheeks and onto the knuckles of the fingers in my mouth. I tried as my stomach and body jerked but held on.

I can't even succeed at this.

Wheezy

What the hell did I just sign up for?!

I close my laptop and settle into the cushion of my loveseat.

I am not a runner. I have asthma. I only run when something is chasing me or while trying to catch the train. Running has always felt like punishment.

So, clearly, a logical thing for me to do is to register for a long-distance race. *Clearly.*

* * *

Somehow, I had found my way to the website for the Rock 'n' Roll Running Series, and I was looking for a race to join.

There are musical acts along the course? Awesome. That'll keep me motivated.

Distance? Let's be realistic. I'm not running anybody's 26.2 miles. I will register for a half marathon. 13.1 miles.

Location? I choose Chicago because the race website describes the route as "flat and fast." Besides, I've always wanted to visit Chicago. I can get a tour while I survive a half marathon. I learn this will be the inaugural Rock 'n' Roll Half Marathon in Chicago. I will be a part of history!

After my excitement about Chicago deep dish pizza wanes, my brain returns me to the present.

Danielle, did you really just register for a half marathon?! On purpose? Yes. Yes, you did.

* * *

The teasing was relentless. The instigator and worst offender was the physical education teacher for my athletic conditioning class during my sophomore year volleyball season. Coach Stevens was a tall, imposing man with a booming voice that was always armed with a snarky comment. He would joke at students' expense, but he seemed to like picking on me most.

As the class ran laps, I was always the last person on the track. Some students could run the miles without stopping; I had an intermittent jogging and walking strategy. I would hustle the best I could during the jogging portion, then when I felt my lungs protest, I would stop jogging and walk. Repeat.

Each lap, Coach Stevens would stand by the edge of the track waiting for me to approach. He'd hike up his shorts, crouch down, and lean close to me as I passed him.

"Come on, Wheezy!" he would yell, while dramatically clapping his hands in my direction. I did not find this funny.

Every day: "Wheezy!" Soon, my classmates and people who weren't even in my class were calling me Wheezy.

One day, I came home after practice extremely annoyed and told my dad what happened. My dad was livid.

"Asthma's not a joke. I ought to give this so-called coach a piece of my mind."

"No, it's okay. I'll handle it," I quickly replied.

I'd seen what happens when my dad gave people a piece of his mind. Sometimes a piece of his mind looked more like the entirety of his open hand or fist.

My dad was right, though. Lung disease—which is what asthma is— is not a joke. A classmate of mine from middle school died at age 14 due to an asthma attack while out skateboarding with friends. Definitely not a joke.

* * *

I am a good student. I register for *Runner's World* magazine. I research the best training and nutrition tips, increments for when to fuel with chews and bars. When to hydrate. Go to the running supply store and have them help me select a pair of $120 running shoes. Pricey, but it's okay. I'm a serious runner; I have all of the equipment and the tips.

I research half marathon training plans and find one for my starting activity level (sitting on the couch) and the amount of time I have to train (13 weeks). I decide which day of the week will be my long-run day (Saturday).

I will start each week with a cross-training day, so I will use the gym in my apartment building to use the elliptical machine, or I'll do some strength training or home workouts. Ease myself into it. I can do this.

I make an agreement with this training plan that when it reads "run," what it really means is "run-walk." I cannot run any significant (or even insignificant) distance without stopping to walk. The plan begins with shorter distances then gradually increases the number of miles each week as your endurance builds. The plan goes as follows:

- Monday: What this plan calls an "easy" run (between two to four miles). Easy to whom?
- Tuesday: Recovery/cross-training day
- Wednesday: Medium run (between three to seven miles)
- Thursday: "Easy" run (between two to four miles)
- Friday: Recovery/cross-training day
- Saturday: Long run (between four to 10 miles)
- Sunday: Recovery (I refuse to do anything on Sundays)

I review the plan and fill in the details on some monthly calendar sheets I'd printed out. Then, panic.

"Oh my god! I don't run the complete distance at any point during this training. So, I'm supposed to just show up on race day and *assume* I can do it?!"

I consult the internet to make sure this is accurate. It is, according to the experts. Your body needs enough time to recover so you and your body don't begin the race already fatigued.

Fine. I accept this thing I cannot change. I had, for some reason, decided to register for a half marathon. And I did so without thinking about the realities of a half marathon.

After reading more details about the race, I learn that the race has a cut-off time—a time limit by which all participants must cross the finish line. The cut-off time is three and a half hours.

Goal: Finish in less than three hours.

Then I read further. The language on the website is very firm and tells me that runners and walkers must pass race checkpoints at miles nine and 11 by a certain time or else they won't be allowed to complete the race. Runners and walkers must maintain a stay-in-the-race pace lest they be picked up by a shuttle and transported to the finish line.

I feel attacked.

~~Goal: Finish in less than three hours.~~

Goal: Not be picked up by the Shame Shuttle and dropped off at the finish line.

* * *

Race morning, I somehow have the presence of mind to write in my journal. I want to write a blog post chronicling my feat so my audience of four people can experience this moment with me.

It's 5:20 am. I totally look the part. I have my race outfit on, complete with a hydration belt around my waist with a pouch holding my inhaler and energy chews. On my arm, an armband with my phone and hotel key. On one shoe, a shoe wallet holding my ID, and on the other, the timing chip tied into my shoelaces. My race bib (number 16210) attached to my front. I am eating a protein bar. I am such a runner.

Stomach is in knots... The race begins at 6:30.

5:24. Going downstairs in about 20 minutes. Stomach in knots. Did I say that already???

* * *

Bodies surround me on all sides. The race organizers sort participants into pace groups based on expected running pace or estimated finish time. Each pace group is gathered in a specific corral. The corral system helps to stagger the start times so thousands of people don't rush ahead at once. The runners in the corrals closest to the starting line are those with the fastest expected pace or shortest estimated finish time.

From my corral, I can't even see the starting line. Here, though, I am amongst my people: the slow runners and the run-walkers. A slow runner or run-walker next to me tells me that we are in "ideal" conditions. Low humidity and no wind in the Windy City.

The corrals release in waves. After what feels like forever, I begin.

I check my pace timing, and I hydrate and take endurance chews at my predetermined intervals. I wave at each of the bands and some supporters as I pass.

At some point during the race, I notice a man. What catches my attention, I believe, is that he is shirtless and is more gray hair than skin. Gray hair everywhere: head, chest, arms, and legs. What keeps my attention is how he moves. Steady. Graceful. His arms swing rhythmically, as if he is swimming through the air. I am captivated.

I also notice that we are around the same pace.

"As long as I keep up with Frank, I am fine," I say. I don't know his actual name, but he looks like a Frank.

I concentrate on not falling on my face and take in the amazing scenery. I run through the city, going over bridges and along the water. I pass many of Chicago's historic landmarks—Soldier Field, Shedd Aquarium, The Field Museum, the Chicago Waterfront. After taking the turn just past mile eight, I am running along the water, enjoying the skyline.

When I return my attention to the road, I notice that Frank is a little too far ahead of me.

"I need to keep up with Frank!" Stay-in-the-race pace.

* * *

At mile 11, my legs start to protest, and I don't think I'll make it. I begin looking at patches of grass where I can desert myself and my goal.

Ooh...that spot looks nice! I can probably just tuck and roll my way over there and curl up so I won't get trampled.

Then, I remember.

Girl. You did not register for runner magazines, buy $120 running shoes, running socks, endurance chews, a hydration belt, a sports watch, shorts, and all of this other gear to give up. You did not spend the last three months of your life getting up at 5:00 a.m. almost every day to run-walk all those damn miles to give up. You did not travel all the way to Chicago to give up.

As I'm having this conversation with myself, two women run beside me. Apparently, I'm not the only one struggling with mile 11.

"This isn't hard! You know what's hard?! Cancer! Cancer is hard!" says one woman to the other.

I look at the women, trying to understand the relationship between them. If the screaming woman is the struggling woman's friend, I really want the struggling woman to get a new friend. If the screaming woman is a coach? Ditto. What a way to talk to a person. Judgment and comparative suffering as a motivational strategy?

In this moment, I think of Coach Stevens.

What *really* motivated me to register for this race? Was there a part of me who wanted to say, "Coach Stevens, Wheezy completed a half marathon!"? Even so, he wouldn't be around to hear me. I haven't seen the man for almost a decade, and I am certain he has not thought of me nearly as often as I have thought of him, if at all.

So, I won't think about him anymore.

Instead, I think about my body and her resilience. How six years ago, she was collapsed on a bathroom floor. And here she is, strong and nourished, doing something I never thought her capable.

I think of myself at age 16, the last one on the track. *If she could only see me now.*

Regardless of my motivation to begin, I decide I will not quit.

Just two more miles. My legs can carry me two more miles.
As I cross the finish line, my hands meet the sky.

Some Accounting

13.1: number of miles "run"

39.3: approximate number of times I thought: "What was I thinking signing up for this race?!"

1: number of celebratory beers drank in the beer garden. Thanks to a beer company sponsor, all finishers are entitled to two complimentary cold beers. It's like 10:00 a.m., and I don't drink beer, but I am sweaty, thirsty, and have just completed a half marathon. I am having one beer. I wonder if it's true what folks say, "Beer never tastes better than after 13.1 miles." I take a sip. No. Beer still tastes bad.

0: number of times I fell out on the ground

0: number of times my feet stopped moving

0: number of times I gave up

* * *

Later, I review my results:

- Finish: 2:55:10
- Pace: 13:22
- Overall: 12742 out of 14459
- Women: 7923 out of 9355
- F 25-29: 2358 out of 2588

12,742nd place out of 14,459 runners and run-walkers!

Nice.

I was not last.

Maybe Wheezy began this race, but Danielle finished it.

Body Image

CW: Specific disordered eating behaviors and body image disturbance

On Friday, April 15, 2016, my body was still recovering from the impacts of a health condition that I developed in winter 2015 that had caused me to lose a lot of weight very quickly. That year, my weight fell to 122 pounds; at 5'9," I was solidly underweight. I was a size two, bordering on size one. I know this because I *almost* fit into a pair of size one jeans; I hated how much I loved that I could almost fit a size one.

One day, I stood at my bathroom mirror, facing my 122-pound body.

What was there? My prominent clavicle. The thigh gap that would not disappear no matter how tightly I squeezed my feet together.

What was not there? The little belly pooch that I have had since the beginning of time. My breasts, the flesh on my thighs I had always hated, any hint of a behind.

I was skeletal. At the height of my eating disorder, this is how I wanted to look. Except, I wanted to be even thinner.

And I wanted to lose seven more pounds than this, I thought. My eyes scanned each inch of my body from my face to my shins. Then I caught my eyes in the mirror.

"Girl, you need to gain some weight!"

* * *

On Friday, April 15, 2016, I lay on the table of a whole-body scanner as the machine analyzed my body's soft tissue and bone composition. I had scheduled this Body Composition Analysis for no reason whatsoever other than my obsession with my body and what percentage of my body was fat and muscle.

At a doctor's appointment shortly after, my doctor asked, "Why did you have a Body Composition Analysis?"

Crap. Well, for one, I didn't think you'd find out.

"I was just curious about my fat and muscle ratio," I say, trying to mirror the nonchalance in her voice.

As she scrolls through my patient record, I hear a quiet "Hmm" from behind the computer screen. My doctor is aware of my history of disordered eating. Her silence is not silent.

* * *

On Friday, April 15, 2016, the body scanner tool captured and delivered a Body Composition Report along with an X-ray image of my body. That image is the silhouette on the cover of this book.

At the time of the Body Composition Analysis, I was 134 pounds.

I chose to use the image of my body on the cover because my body has been so central to who I am. I wanted to put front and center the body that I have tried to erase and conceal for most of my life.

The image also represents me at a point in my life when I had lost weight—because of illness and not due to my interference—and then became obsessed with the physical outcome of that illness.

On Friday, April 15, 2016, I was a woman who had "recovered" from her eating disorder.

* * *

I have no concept of how my body naturally looks. In the past seven years, my weight has existed in a space between 122 to 190 pounds. Among other things, illness, emotions, and depression explain the losses and gains. I carry my emotions on my body. I eat when I'm stressed and can't eat when I'm heartbroken. While in my relationship with Matt, I experienced depression to a degree I hadn't since college. Toward the end of our relationship, I was shocked to learn that I was 190 pounds. As part of my eating disorder recovery, I didn't own a scale, so I was unaware of how much weight I had gained over the past year and a half. When we met, I was 145 pounds, which my body seemed always to find its way back to.

My TEDx Talk was about two months after the incident described in "The Door Frame." As I mentioned in my talk, I had been concerned about my weight. What didn't make the script is that the weight I carried was from the physical and emotional impacts of that relationship.

In January 2021, I experienced a life-upending event that resulted in grief and a diagnosis of PTSD. As I write this, less than a year has passed, and I haven't been able to process it in a way that I can write about it just yet. But I can tell you a bit about the aftermath.

In the weeks immediately after, I had no appetite at all. I couldn't tolerate any food, so I lost weight. Then, after a few months had passed, the emotional eating surfaced. I gave myself permission to eat what felt good because I wanted to feel something good. So, I ate what required little effort, which often took the form of convenient, comfort foods like pizza and french fries.

One day, I needed to concentrate on something other than my grief, so I baked a cake. The amount of precision required for baking is excellent for distraction. To weigh the flour by the ounce, to notice the consistency of the batter to avoid over- or under-mixing. From a list of ingredients emerged a two-layer cake with a compote in the middle and a cream cheese frosting. I divided the cake into sixteen slices, then wrapped fifteen of them in plastic wrap, and put the slices in the freezer "for the future." But what happened is that I ate cake every day after that. On my most challenging day, I ate a slice of cake after each meal and snack—four slices of cake in one day. Weight gain.

After five months of feeling wholly out of control, I needed structure. I wanted to lose 20 pounds, to return to my familiar 145 pounds. So, I signed up for a popular app to help me lose weight. I like behavioral neuroscience, so I was fascinated by their approach. While not required to track my calorie intake, I did. I convinced myself I would be okay. I was only tracking my calories to learn what portions look like.

One morning, I found myself picking individual dried cranberries out of my oatmeal because I accidentally served myself 11 grams instead of 10 grams. As with most things I do, I became obsessive in my approach. I was allowed to eat 28 grams of raw almonds, not 29 grams.

I knew this was not a path I wanted to tread, so I messaged my coach.

"Hey, I noticed this program relies on calorie tracking, and that has the potential to lead me to an obsessive place," my message began.

I didn't tell her that I was already in that obsessive place. I didn't tell her about the cranberries.

When I began writing this book, I was still in the program. Then an interesting thing happened. I started forgetting to log into the app to complete the daily lessons and track my meals. When I noticed that trend, I considered my options: (1) I could spend time logging my meals down to the individual walnut, or (2) I could spend time writing, which I have not given myself permission to pursue for most of my life. I eventually stopped logging into the app altogether. Instead of spending time obsessing about how much of myself I might be able to diminish, I became obsessed with the process of creation.

For almost 30 years, I have fixated on changing my body. I am 37 years old. I have missed *so much* of my life.

Imagine if I had channeled that energy elsewhere. Imagine what I could've accomplished. My single-minded pursuit of maintaining and concealing an eating disorder required me to access and tax my mental, physical, and emotional functions. In the years since, I have scrutinized, criticized, dieted, and exercised my body to move closer to an ever-evolving ideal. Imagine if I had devoted that focus, time, and attention to detail to building a business, becoming fluent in French, learning to dance Cuban Salsa or play the piano, or doing literally anything else.

* * *

Today, it's easy for me to say, "I won't restrict my calories, over-exercise, or purge anymore."

A more difficult thing to say: "When I look into the mirror, I will not wish my body away. I will not look at each aspect of myself, limb by limb, and wish it were different."

The first concerns my behavior, and the other concerns my beliefs. After that day on the floor in my bathroom, I stopped the behaviors, but the beliefs about myself and my body remained.

The Body Composition Analysis analyzes the body in terms of its components. I've decided to complete my own analysis. But instead of thinking of components such as fat mass and lean tissue mass, I contemplate my mind's relationship to my body.

As a child, my mind learned that I had a body. Then, my mind became exposed to stories from various storytellers. My mind learned that the body I had was imperfect and deviant. My mind learned that I needed to hide my body. My mind learned there were consequences for having a Black, female body and doing radical things with it such as existing, breathing, walking, standing in line, and sitting.

My mind then began telling its own stories and providing commentary for my body. As my body walked through the world, my mind created the story that my body was an inconvenience: "I'm sorry this body showed up with these thighs. I'm sorry this body is the best I could do. I'm sorry this body showed up wrong and a total mess." My body enrolled at a new school; my mind believed she needed to apologize that the body that showed up in the classroom was Black. My mind tells my body she is flawed. My mind silences my body when she speaks and asks for nourishment and care.

But here's the thing. *My body existed first.* My body predates my mind's knowledge of what a body even *is.* My body predates my mind's awareness of Blackness. My Black body predates my mind's understanding that some other minds perceive that Blackness is inferior. My body is inferior to nothing. My body is infinitely wiser than my mind.

My body is not a project. She is, simply, what is.

* * *

August 9, 2019

The first day after I am discharged from the hospital and am no longer receiving a steady stream of pain meds through an IV, my body begins to talk to me. I believe I can hear her now because she has raised her voice and is very persistent.

She says, "Why did you do this to me?! Every possible position I can take is unbearable. A pain unlike any I have ever experienced. And, just to confirm, you're going to do this to me *again*?"

She speaks to me this way every day.

And then, around day 10, her tone of voice changes.

"Hmm...this isn't as bad as I thought it would be. I can handle this. But remember what the nurse told you. Let my pain be your guide. Maintain your pain medication schedule. Stay ahead of the pain, don't chase it. By the time I feel the pain, it's a bit too late."

What follows is weeks of my body and I learning how to navigate the world together.

From the walker, I transition to two crutches. Then one. Then a cane. Then just the support of my unassisted self.

I wait three months, then undergo the surgery to remove my left hip joint's damaged bone and tissue and replace them with the same stainless steel, cobalt chrome, and titanium implant that now lives in my right hip joint. The process is the same, but this time, just a one-night stay in the hospital and a bit less fear.

Today, two years since my surgeries, people still ask, "Does it feel like you have implants? Can you tell the difference?"

No. My truth is I feel what the misinterpreted X-ray once told me was true: normal alignment, normal bones in the pelvis, and normal hip joints.

I do walk the world differently now, though.

My AVN diagnosis made me think—for the first time—of my body in terms of function. Through my experience with my hip surgeries, I learned the anatomy of my bones. I had never bothered to understand the purpose that my bones, muscle, nerve tissues, and organs served.

Why does my body exist?

Through reading about nutrition, I've learned why my body needs fat...and food. I practically considered sleep an inconvenience until I learned that sleep impacts everything from brain function to our immune system. Through my mindful self-compassion practice, I learned about the default mode network in the brain that is most active at rest, which explains why my mind wanders when I'm trying to do a mindfulness exercise. While I thought I had "failed" at mindfulness, my brain was doing precisely what it was *designed* to do.

As with most everything, I needed to understand the body *intellectually* before I simply allowed it to be.

* * *

18 June 2019

Sixteen years ago, I was 19 years old, collapsed on the floor of the bathroom in our house. I was tired of starving myself, tired of throwing up, tired of being hungry. Even then, I picked myself up from the floor. I have a history of picking myself up. I need to do that for myself right now.

I was nineteen years old when I purged for the final time. The perceivable evidence that I no longer have an eating disorder is that I no longer restrict calories, purge, abuse laxatives, or over-exercise. That day on the bathroom floor, I stopped trying to disappear my body because it hurt physically.

Then it hurt in other ways. I felt like a failure. I was no longer adept at making my body do what I forced her to do. I never thought maybe she didn't have more to give. While I was upset that my body was holding onto nourishment, she was concerned with keeping me alive. She was doing her job, and I was angry with her for it. Maybe she had finally had enough of my trying to control how she did her job.

So, I surrender. I'm tired of fighting with my body. I'm tired of using my body as a canvas for my emotions. I am, simply, tired. I want her to take over from here. I've learned that she already seems to know what she's doing.

Recovery

CW: *Disordered eating, body image disturbance; references to sexualized violence and abuse*

September 13, 2013

Today, I had a phone exchange with a nurse from my doctor's office. I called the office because I was prescribed a new medication and, as I was reading the medication guide, I noticed a warning: "USE OF THIS MEDICINE IS NOT RECOMMENDED if you have a history of an eating disorder (e.g., anorexia, bulimia)." After I identified myself and shared the reason I was calling, I said, "I'm a recovering bulimic. It's been at least a decade since I've purged, but I still struggle with body dysmorphic disorder." I didn't even flinch.

I realized something recently. I will always be in recovery.

Three months, 12 days after stepping off the TEDx stage, I wrote that blog post. Since writing the post, I began to better understand how labeling myself as "bulimic" or as having "body dysmorphic disorder" didn't capture my experience (for the latter, the more accurate term is "body image disturbance"). While in the throes of my eating disorder (1998–2003), I only knew of two eating disorders: anorexia and bulimia; I didn't fit the diagnostic criteria for either. In looking at the *Diagnostic and Statistical Manual of Mental Disorders* now, there is so much new language that hadn't been available to me before: Other Specified Feeding or Eating Disorders, Atypical Anorexia Nervosa, Purging Disorder. I feel, at once, relief that my experience is finally accounted for and legitimized and dismay that I find belonging in those pages.

* * *

The most concise way I've come to understand AVN: the cause of the condition is gradual tissue death due to disrupted blood supply. The weakening tissue alters the bone's structural integrity, and microfractures begin to form in the bone, which results in the bone's eventual death and collapse.

When I finally understood what had been happening to my body, I felt grief. I thought about how my body was suffering, but I didn't know. I remembered how I used to stand in front of the mirror and look at my body, running my hands over my thighs to touch the "excess" fat I wanted to erase.

Weeks after my final surgery, I stood in front of the mirror, looking at my body as I often did. As I traced my fingers over my surgical scars, I spoke to my body with a gentleness I had never offered her before.

"I am *so* sorry. I am so sorry I didn't know."

For how long had my bones been dying?

When did I become so unrecognizable to myself? Might it have been an accumulation of experiences just subtle enough to escape my notice?

A gradual death—of bone, of self. A death occurring silently but undetected by the mind. A steady weakening until there is too much damage for the structure to remain intact.

Microfractures—*traumas* some might call them—did alter me to my core. Some of them, while painful, were rather easily addressed. Have a surgery (or two), learn to walk again.

But others?

Eating disorder, which is the gradual erasure of the physical self wherein the body is the target of the mind. Sexualized violence, during which a body is violated, and then additional violence comes in the aftermath when we are doubted, dismissed, or are led to believe the violation is somehow our fault or responsibility. Internalized oppression, which is the learned denial or erasure of culture and heritage that results in a loss of history, identity, and belonging. Abuse, which often goes unrecognized, or, when recognized, we rationalize why the behavior is not *exactly* okay, but we will allow space for it. Transgenerational trauma, which is often passed down as an inheritance, via oral tradition, or by observation.

Do we ever recover from these microfractures, these traumas, or do we simply learn to walk with them?

Hands

CW: Describes an attempted act of sexualized violence depicted in film

I am sitting on the couch with my sister watching a movie. The movie details the transformation of a young woman who is deaf but just recently learned to communicate with sign language.

At the end of a date, her male companion drives them in his truck to a secluded location and parks. As he leans in for a kiss, the woman backs away and signs to tell him she wants to go home. He replies that he needs something from her before he takes her home, and he leans closer. Despite her resistance, he becomes more insistent and tries to take the encounter further. As he moves closer to her, her hands protest furiously.

"She's trying to sign her way out of being raped?" My sister's voice breaks the silence in the room.

A question and an exclamation. I've never heard an interrobang used so skillfully.

"Well, what do you expect her to do?" I ask.

"She could've used her hands to fight him off instead of signing."

I turn back to the TV and to the scene.

But...isn't she still fighting?

An Education

When I wrote my first bio for a publication, I followed the format that I understood to be the norm: "Danielle Shontae Smith holds an MA in English–Creative Writing from Western Washington University, as well as a BA in Women's Studies from UCLA, with emphases in social inequality and literature. A student affairs professional by trade, Danielle currently writes and seeks a poetry community in Bellingham, WA."

The language didn't feel quite right to me, but I didn't know what other language I could use to write my bio because I had no model.

When we talk about educations, the language is so passive. Taylor *obtained* her BA from University of Pennsylvania. Maya *has* an MA from Howard University. Michelle *holds* a PhD from University of Chicago.

When I read a person's educational background and see the words "has," "holds," and "obtained," I sigh.

So...Michelle, you were just standing on a corner one day when someone strolled by and handed you a PhD, and now you're just holding it? Claim what's yours, Michelle!

I wonder how their biographies would read if they were to share the truth about the life they lived while they studied for their degrees.

* * *

Danielle Shontae Smith earned an MA in English–Creative Writing from Western Washington University; a BA in Women's Studies from UCLA, with emphases in social inequality and literature; and an AA with Great Distinction in Humanities & Fine Arts from Riverside Community College.

Between her AA, BA, and MA, Danielle successfully completed 61 classes in seven years while battling crippling depression; an eating disorder; impostor syndrome; sleep deprivation to study, lesson plan, and grade assignments; several breakdowns; sexual harassment; racial microaggressions; intimate partner violence; housing, food, and financial insecurity, including selling her plasma so she could afford food until she was told she could no longer donate plasma because her iron and protein levels were too low because she was nutritionally deficient from having no nutritive food; and living for several years in a city that consistently tops the list of places in the U.S. that get the least days of sunshine.

Danielle has since returned to her native Southern California and is putting her learned marketable skills to use at a full-time, grown-up job so her rescue dog can have a nice life.

Pretty solid first draft.

For Your Information

"How do I *feel*?"

Why can I not answer? I look down at the handout that will allegedly help me identify my emotions.

While I can't identify my original emotion, I can say for sure that my therapist's question has caused me to feel *flummoxed.*

I am a spelling bee champion! I *know* words. The language of emotion, however, is not one in which I am proficient. I *feel* a lot of emotions. Do I know exactly what emotion I'm feeling or how to articulate my emotions in an "x happened; therefore, I feel y" format? No. I can write you a poem about the experience *around* the feeling, though.

Of the eight primary emotions on this handout, I identify most with anger, guilt, and sadness. Every. Time.

* * *

I am old enough to remember a time before GPS and navigation software. Instead of navigation apps, there were maps. Whenever I travel and stay in a hotel, one of my favorite activities is to peruse the display in the lobby that features maps, sightseeing guides, and other materials. I like reading about the various local adventures that I could experience, if only I could afford it (wine tours) or had fewer phobias (any activity on or in a body of water). I collect some maps and booklets to look at while my traveling companion drives. Then the fun stops. I cannot over-estimate how quickly I can go from calmly scanning local points of interest to a profanity-laced temper tantrum when I try to return a map to its formerly folded self. No matter how closely I follow its lines, I cannot refold it *precisely* as it was before. I simply cannot remember which folds I unfolded in what order. So, I fight with the insubordinate map—competitive and determined to win.

Stubborn! Refuses to comply! I respect these traits, but this is not what I need from a map.

I followed your damn *lines! How are you not a perfect rectangle by now?!*

At times, I accept help. Once, I was fighting with a map while traveling with a boyfriend. After watching me for a few minutes, he asked if he could help. I shoved the disobedient document at him. He took the map from my hands. I blinked, and when my eyes opened, there it was anew: rectangle, crisp corners. He handed the folded map over to me.

His lips said nothing, but his look asked, "Why was that so hard?"

I will take the map, but I will leave the judgment. Besides, my thorough internet search tells me that I am not the only one who is so afflicted.

* * *

I suppose the question to ask is why anyone would be so affected because a piece of paper will not return to a perfect rectangle with crisp corners. I suppose the assumption here is that such a person is dealing with misdirected or repressed emotions.

One downside of having two artificial hips: my surgeon advised against high-impact activities. No running? No argument there. But, alas, no kickboxing. I must find a low-impact way to manage my rage.

These days, the reality of my daily life is that I encounter fewer travel maps and more medication information leaflets.

Unfold and read the Patient Information leaflet for the new prescription. Try to follow the lines to refold it. *Use your acquired coping strategies. Try a deep breath or three. Pause. Try again. Slower and more deliberately this time. Breathe.*

I'm still competitive, but now the fight comes with fewer casualties.

Critical Personal Narrative

"I mean, I read the chapters...I just don't think I'm that hard on myself," I say flipping through the workbook.

When I look up from my lap, my therapist is just *looking* at me. Her mouth says nothing. But her expression takes a tone with me: "That's cute. I'll give you a moment to think through what you just said."

I look back at my workbook. According to the self-compassion assessment, my self-compassion is low.

* * *

In 2015, I attended a week-long diversity, equity, and inclusion institute for educators. In one of the breakout sessions, the facilitators assigned us to write a critical personal narrative, an exercise they assigned to their high school students. I don't remember the prompt or how exactly the facilitators described what a critical personal narrative was, but the way I remember it was that we were to write about experiences that shaped us into the people we are today. But we were not to just write the story; we were to reflect on the story we tell, including any individuals who were involved and their impact on who we are.

After the institute ended, the participants and trainers celebrated together at a reception. During the reception, one of the facilitators and I had a lovely conversation. We shared stories. He talked to me about his daughter who was around my age; I told him about George. Before we parted, we exchanged email addresses. I was sure to warn him that my email response time is abysmal. He said not to worry; I would reply when I was ready. He wrote me shortly after our meeting. As I considered my response, I thought it would be nice to share with him my critical personal narrative—the product of the workshop that his team hosted. I closed his email with a plan to reply soon. My critical personal narrative wasn't quite right. I needed to revise it a bit. I would wait to reply until the piece that didn't yet have a name was perfect.

As with much of what I wrote at the time, my critical personal narrative took shape as a poem. I revised the poem. Months passed. Revision. *I really want to reply to his email.* Revision. There is progress, but now there is guilt. Years pass. Revision. *I really need to reply to his email.* Revision. *Is it too late to reply to his email?* To guilt, I add embarrassment. Revision. *Will he even remember me? Will he care? I am the literal worst.* Hello, shame.

I was still revising my critical personal narrative when I included it in this book. More than six years have passed since he wrote me on Monday, June 29, 2015. I have been revising this poem for more than six years. *Six years.* Because I wanted a piece of text to be perfect. Not only is perfection an impossible goal, but perfection was not at all the assignment. Six years of guilt, embarrassment, and shame that I unnecessarily held, as no one asked me to carry them. Six years of the mental clutter of an unattended item on my to-do list. Imagine the weight.

In the spirit of honoring the person who is writing this book, I decided to be brave and reply. I crave the feeling of achievement and satisfaction that I would get by telling you I actually sent the email; however, as I write this, my email response sits in my Drafts folder, awaiting a bit more bravery from its author. In my response, I ask for nothing in return, no need to reply, but perhaps a pause to acknowledge the human in me who—like her text—has been a perpetual work in progress. When I do press "Send," I will share the poem with him: "On Consoling Men Who Cry." The poem that began its life over six years ago as a draft of a critical personal narrative in a conference room in a workshop that he hosted. I will let him know that I am writing a book that sounds a whole lot like a critical personal narrative.

* * *

Before society, religion, etc. got ahold of us, who were we? Before we knew we were black or that a certain grade of hair was considered "good," who were we?

I don't know if I remember a time before *any* of it.

"Why don't you like yourself?" My mom's question at the TEDx reception.

Until recently, I didn't believe that choice was ever mine.

What's to like? To like yourself, you must know yourself. I didn't even know who I was. I was a poseable doll waiting for directions: What do you need from me? Who do I need to be in this moment?

I have experienced a lifetime of societal messaging telling me that I am nothing.

And then, I am shamed or questioned for believing I am nothing.

* * *

About six years ago, my office hosted an event for students led by an amazing speaker, Michael McGill, Jr. His talk to students concerned self-love, self-esteem, and the need for us to understand our worth, value, and identity.

Again, there I was: the advisor and instructor taking copious notes. I nodded along, trying to look like a professional whose interest was purely intellectual. I hoped that anyone observing my frenzied notetaking would believe I was capturing material to share with my students.

After the presentation, Michael and I walked and talked. During our conversation, I told him some of the thoughts his talk inspired in me. As he spoke, I had thought of how I had, over the years, considered getting braces to straighten my teeth. The way my teeth naturally took shape in my mouth—with a gap between my two front teeth—has been the subject of teasing for most of my life.

Michael stopped in his tracks.

"Don't you *dare* straighten your teeth!"

After his visit, we kept in touch. Over the years, in various messages, Michael has written to me:

> "Your teeth represent the queen that you are and God's fingerprint on your smile."
>
> "Your teeth are your unique layer of beauty, and they declare wealth in other cultures."

I looked it up. Various cultures and communities have associated a gap between one's front teeth with wealth, beauty, good luck, fertility, or even a healthy sexual appetite. One story tells me that my teeth are flawed and need to be fixed. A different story tells me that my teeth are a symbol of good fortune. We're surrounded by stories all the time. I had chosen to listen to the wrong storytellers.

Humans have teeth so we can eat food. As my teeth allow me to eat food, my teeth serve their function. Therefore, I don't need to invest thousands of dollars to "fix" them. Doing so would be purely aesthetic.

But more than anything, it's kind of hard to justify modifying your teeth when someone tells you that your teeth—just as they are—represent your nobility.

* * *

For most of my life, I haven't had much of a life. Rather, I have had a series of projects. I made a lot of promises to myself along the way, saying, "I will be happy when..."

No. I wouldn't.

I thought living in California was making me miserable, so I moved. Then I was miserable, cold, and vitamin D deficient in Washington for 10 years. If I thought a job was just the worst, I got a new job. Then I was miserable but with a new job title and a different office. I was miserable being single, so I entered a relationship. I was miserable in a relationship, so I left it.

Different weight? Different weather? Different boss? No, no, and no.

I get it! I see what I did wrong. Life feels unmanageable because I have the wrong organizational system. I need a new strategy.

So, I attended the webinars, read the articles, learned the strategies, downloaded the productivity apps, bought the planners and the right pens, the action-oriented notepads, sticky notes, and journals. Unlined journals, dotted journals. The 0.7 mm gel pens in a rainbow of colors. Took an assessment to understand my time perspective.

Then I looked around me. *I have all of the proper tools and strategies. Why does everything still feel so impossible?*

I have learned that I can be miserable anywhere, at any weight, in any state, in any weather, and with any organizational system or productivity strategy.

I had believed there was an answer somewhere. I just needed to find it. I hadn't found the right formula or strategy, hadn't tried hard enough, hadn't *thought* hard enough. I believed there was a point when I would...*arrive*. I'd be a fully optimized human. My life would run so effortlessly because I had created all of the necessary systems for it to do so and had accounted for everything, all contingencies. My life would run like my bills operate on autopay: seamless.

But all of these annoying obstacles kept getting in the way. Sleep. Each successive job that would be perfect "if only...." Romantic partners whose imperfect human selves disrupt the carefully crafted storyline. The conversations with dear friends and family that force an acknowledgement of the impermanence of life. Medical conditions that are idiopathic, with no cure and no answers beyond "we'll keep an eye on it."

I was today years old when I realized that what I have been calling "obstacles," other people call...*life*.

I never questioned if the fully optimized human that I sought to be was actually achievable. All that mattered was that I *believed* it was, and therefore, I was a failure for not being so. I never stopped to consider that my belief might be flawed. No. *I* was flawed.

Not only did I believe there was a finish line, but my problem was I assumed the perfection I sought was at the end of it.

* * *

After I completed the half marathon, I needed a break, so I gave myself the gift of one full month of no running. After the month passed, I put on the same outfit I wore on race day (for inspiration and nostalgia), tied my running shoes, buckled my hydration belt around my waist, and headed out the door on an "easy" run.

I struggled to complete one mile.

What happened? Why is this so hard?!

I dragged myself home and sat on my couch. New training plan: "How to go from completing a half marathon to sitting on your couch in one month." I had somehow let myself forget how I had gotten myself to the half marathon in the first place. I had to start slowly, build my endurance and my muscle strength. But now, I had no desire to start that training all over again. Too much work to start from the beginning. I never ran again.

I wish I had held onto this lesson of how quickly I could lose progress in practically everything if I don't dedicate myself to maintaining it.

I had tried to create an almost automated life—one complete with a complex system of strategies and tools that required the initial hard work to create but then would be hands-off in the process. I needed this self-regulating approach because I found life to be so exhausting. I believed that if I just created a system in which my life just *worked*, I wouldn't have to put in more, well, work.

My identity and self-worth were malleable and determined by others around me. Because I believed I needed to earn attention and care, I didn't challenge or disagree with people close to me. I had developed no boundaries. I shied away from conflict. I didn't know how to identify my emotions or needs, let alone understand how to express them. I learned to hide (sometimes literally) when confronted with a situation that was too emotionally difficult to bear. When I encountered struggle, pain, or loss—like the terminal diagnosis and eventual death of a loved one—I tried to put as much distance as I could between me and the experience of having to acknowledge and feel it. I believed I could avoid or outsmart conflict, pain, and hardship.

I didn't cultivate the skills to engage with my life.

I had been seeking perfection, which is unattainable. I had sought external validation, which always left me disappointed because external approval is so precarious. Human beings are difficult to please and their expectations and criteria for approval always seem to shift. So, I would adjust then wonder, "Am I good enough *now*?" I had been acting for so long, putting up a façade and trying to be the person that others wanted me to be.

No wonder I was so overwhelmed.

When I finally confronted my best frenemies, Intellection, Striving, and Achievement, I told myself that they didn't define who I was or determine my worth. I treated that declaration as a lesson learned, something I checked off the list on my path to recovery from perfectionism and people-pleasing. The overachiever in me attempted to unlearn a lifetime's worth of socialization all at once.

I feel as though, for most of my life, I've been at mile 11 of a grueling race looking for exits—a soft place to land where life gets easy.

But life is not that. Becoming a human is as straightforward as being born. Participating in the human experience, however, is a *practice*.

There is no delete button. No autopay, no automation. No such thing as a fully optimized human. I must choose to put one foot in front of the next.

Girl, you didn't come all this way to give up. Your body can carry you so many more miles.

* * *

"Doesn't sound as though you allow yourself much space to be human," my therapist said.

I had just read aloud my responses to some of the reflection questions in chapter one of the *Mindful Self-Compassion Workbook*. Looking at some of the language I used (*I feel like a slight failure, I'm a bit disappointed in myself, Why can't I get it together?!*), she wasn't fully wrong.

Shortly after beginning our therapy relationship, I asked a question that had been lingering in my mind for years.

"Are there people who just stay in therapy and on medication for the rest of their lives?" I asked. I believed I would surely be one of them, as there was something fundamentally flawed about me.

After meeting weekly for five months and hearing an uncensored transcript of my inner dialogue, my therapist introduced me to mindful self-compassion. I ordered the *Mindful Self-Compassion Workbook* ("Ooh, a workbook. I like workbooks!") and began sessions, feeling a bit guarded but also curious. Having started learning mindful self-compassion in July 2021, I'm still new to the practice, so here is an imperfect overview. The core elements of self-compassion are common humanity, mindfulness, and self-kindness. In basic terms, *common humanity* recognizes that all human beings endure hardships, experience failure, and make mistakes, and these shared experiences allow for connection rather than the feeling of isolation that often accompanies struggle; *mindfulness* is being aware of our present moment and facing our truth as it is while viewing our experiences with an objective perspective, rather than judgment; and *self-kindness* is showing care and acceptance toward ourselves rather than criticism.

So...not *exactly* what I've been doing my whole life.

The story I had told myself about myself is this: Failure is not a word in my lexicon. I had been operating under the impression that I alone would be able to discover the secret of a life lived perfectly. *Think harder, find a new strategy, buy some new pens, implement, work harder. Repeat.*

When my efforts inevitably did not result in the perfection I sought, I created a story that my efforts failed because of some inadequacy on my part. And then I would keep trying, all the while saying, "I am *failing* at life!" With striving for perfection, I have much practice. But this new approach, self-compassion? *This sounds like a lot of work,* I remember thinking.

Six months in, I can testify that practicing self-compassion *is* a lot of work, but it is undeniably less taxing than the work I was doing to diminish myself. Instead of laboring every day trying to fix and change myself into something I'm not, I'm learning acceptance and the hard work of leaving myself the hell alone. As challenging as the former was, I feel the latter is infinitely harder.

I don't know this method.

Five sessions into self-compassion, my therapist posed some questions for me to consider until our next meeting: *What if things already work the way they're meant to? What if you just let yourself be okay? How much time do you spend on things that don't matter? How would you spend your time if you weren't on the constant quest to improve yourself?*

The question "What if you just let yourself be okay?" was revolutionary. I'm not sure that it should have been, though.

"So...just...be okay? I'm supposed to walk through the world like there's nothing I need to fix?"

Reflect on that. That's the homework.

I walked out of her office, through the hall, and down the stairs in somewhat of a daze. I had a feeling I couldn't quite place.

Is this...relief? I think I might be feeling relieved.

And then all of my life's problems were solved ~~forever~~ for about five minutes.

Yes, You Can

I

Two women walk by. One woman appears to be in her mid-30s, the other in her early 20s.

"My husband and I have decided not to have children," the older woman says.

The younger woman stops walking and stares at the other, amazed. "You can do that?!"

The older woman laughs and says, "Yeah!"

II.

"What if a student asks a question I don't know the answer to?" I ask. My pen is poised to take notes. The three-inch ring binder with the teaching curriculum is open on my lap. I *refuse* to step foot into a classroom unprepared.

"Just tell them 'You know, I don't know. I'll look into that and get back to you,' then get back to them with the answer," says the Director.

I blink at her.

YOU CAN DO THAT?!

III.

During workshop in our short prose class, a classmate has shared her flash fiction piece, and now our classmates are providing feedback.

"I didn't really connect with this story," says a male classmate.

"Well, you're not my reader," she replies, unperturbed.

My head snaps up from her manuscript.

"Who is your target reader?" It's a common question. I know this.

In writing studies, we call this rhetorical awareness. The writer considers the rhetorical situation of a text: its purpose, audience, stakeholders, and context. When we write, we often begin with setting an intention for the kind of experience we want our reader to have. Who would care about the subject you're writing about? *Why* should they care? When you have a specific reader in mind when you write, you will shape the way you write your text.

I know this as a student *and* as a writing instructor. I have given lectures on this. And still...

I look at her in admiration. Then look to my male classmate and to my professor, waiting for them to react.

To say, "You're not my reader" is to say, "What I have created is not for you; therefore, I will not consider or accept your feedback."

You can say that?! To someone's face?!

IV.

What if...

I disrupt my existing, unhealthy patterns and cultivate new behaviors?

I discard the scripts written for me and write my own?

I stop playing a role and, instead, only allow people in my life who will honor the authentic and unfractured me?

I stop denying my needs and desires to avoid rejection and confrontation with others?

I decide that transgenerational trauma stops with me?

I care more about living in integrity than I do about being liked?

I walk this Earth just as I am and not constantly work to fix myself?

Can I do that?

The Grammar of Me

Have you ever had this experience?

A close friend, relative, or someone else you care about recommends a piece of art to you. Perhaps a poem, book, TV show, or movie. Since you're currently reading a book, I will assume you are a person who reads books. Let's say your dear one recommends a book for you to read.

With their recommendation, did they gush to you about it? Say, "You *must* read this! You'll love it. Trust me."

And then you trust them and read the book, but then feel that you shouldn't have, in fact, trusted them. You hate the book or are underwhelmed by the book. Do you start to wonder if you should trust your friend's judgment? *How am I friends with a person who would love something like this? This is art? How could* anyone *love this?*

You don't want to tell your dear one that you didn't like the book that they recommended to you because you hope not to offend them.

You *wanted* to love the book because they did, and they bothered to recommend it to you.

So, you decide to revisit the book—this thing you didn't love immediately.

You return to the book again and again trying to see what your dear one saw in it.

Did I miss a meaning? Did I miss the symbolism?

You're reading the book with the same eyes, and yet, now you're looking intentionally. You approach the book differently. This time, you're *looking* to love it.

But not just your intention has changed. You're adopting a different, more nuanced way of experiencing the book, *feeling* it. Maybe with each subsequent review of this book, you can offer it insight from having lived a bit more life, gathered more context.

And then it happens.

Maybe it was as you explored the pages of the book, holding its leaves between your fingers...

Maybe it was when you were looking in awe at the breaks of the lines, the layout on the page...

Maybe a sentence you once passed over made you stop and draw in a breath...

Maybe you discovered a word that had once been rendered obsolete but is now experiencing a revival at the author's hands...

Maybe you found a way to work through a troubling passage or sentence...

Maybe you finally understood the title...

And, with this, you see it. *Oh!* That's *what they loved about it. I didn't see it before, but I do now.*

There *is* value here. This *is* art.

Have you ever experienced anything like this?

Revising my relationship with myself through the practice of mindful self-compassion has been a *lot* like that.

On the Surface

Not long after grandma died, I stood in the doorway of your bedroom and watched you.

You, standing in your room near your dresser. You, fighting back tears and wiping a thin layer of dust from the wood. You, tidying the items on the surface.

As I watch you, I am struck by what I've inherited from you. My height, that's certain. But I might have received this from you, too, I think. How I busy my hands as the rest of me disintegrates.

I have seen you be many things: a tower, a wrecking ball.

I realize that now what you are is a boy without his mother.

I didn't realize that you could be this.

* * *

At an October 2021 event on intentional living, a panelist offered an exercise: "If you had just 24 hours to live, how would you spend your time?" *Visit the ocean. Take my dog on the best walk and let her smell all the flowers. Watch the sunset.* I paused, trying to think of more.

Then, a voice from the quiet: *Mend my relationship with my parents.*

As the years passed, I demanded that my parents recognize and respect that I had grown up, but I didn't allow them to. I had suspended my parents in time, granting them no passage beyond the storylines in which I felt most judged, minimized, and silenced by them. The stories I created of my parents never changed. If I am rewriting my story, I need to allow them the same grace. Their stories too deserve revision.

A Few Short Plays to Save the World

"Steve Harper's writing is clean and dirty at the same time and I love that. Structurally his work is sound, his characters are relatable and identifiable but there always seems to be a reality-based factor that believably complicates or sullies that "cleanliness". As an actor, I love it when the dirty is liberally applied. What a great collection of plays for theater students to dig into, both as actors and directors."

-Russell G. Jones
Theater Maker/Facilitator/Collaborator/Actor (*Tommy*)

"Steve Harper's writing has an underlying, yet profound sadness to it. It is powerful in his work and keys into the inherit loneliness that all human beings experience at one time or another."

-Cezar Williams
Actor and Stage Director

"Steve provokes us to look more carefully at systems of race and power and our participation in them in ways that linger long after the blackout."

-Laura Ekstrand
Artistic Director, Vivid Stage

"Steve's work is unexpected. He mines the mystical out of the ordinary and brings the relatable & everyday world face to face with a world of fantastical possibility. Steve is an actor's writer. His writing is as compulsively watchable as it is readable."

-Nick Newell
Director of New Play Development, Lean Ensemble Theatre
Associate Professor of Theatre, Georgia Southern University

"Steve Harper is a thoroughly original, insightful and inquisitive playwright. His plays offer us a highly engaging but twisted look at race relations in America. It's a quality which makes Harper's work unexpected, disruptive and ultimately a fulfilling experience."

-Gregg Daniel
Director/Actor (*Insecure*)/Educator

Hands (Reprise)

CW: Brief mentions of disordered eating behavior and sexualized violence

Isn't she still fighting?

My mother's hand that held her shaking head
the participant ribbon in my hand
Ms. Cagle's hands holding the keychain
the hands that touched me without permission
the fingers I used for purging, trying to erase myself
Coach Stevens's hands clapping at me on the track
the interviewer's hand holding the corner of my résumé
my interviewee hands folded neatly in my lap
a white girl's hand in my hair
the white hands giving me stacks of books

* * *

the woman raising her hand to me in the car
my hands holding the spelling bee trophy
my hands pushing myself up from the floor of the bathroom
my hands meeting the sky after crossing the finish line
a hand grazing my arm in admiration of my Black skin
my mom's right hand holding my shaking, sweating left hand
    until the very moment I was called to the TEDx stage.

I've been thinking a lot about hands and the stories they tell.

dear lucille

white me
and i'm wearing
white history
but there's no future
in those clothes
so i take them off and
wake up
dancing.

- FROM "MY DREAM ABOUT BEING WHITE"
LUCILLE CLIFTON

* * *

CW: Sexualized violence, disordered eating, body image disturbance

dear lucille,

i came to know you from your dreams
may i tell you mine?

lucille, in my dreams:
i am just born, and i am a shield—

my skin impervious
to messaging that will communicate:

danielle, your body is deviance

lucille, i am a prophesier who foresees
my hair texture, the fullness
of my lips, thighs, hips
my brown skin, rich with melanin
the markers of my natural body
will soon become fads, commodities
worth purchase. i know it is a seller's market

and

i do not negotiate
i will not yield

lucille, i am seven years old, and i am aware
of biocultural differences in body composition
i look at seven-year-old girls and honor their bodies
i do not think of seven-year-old girls solely in terms
of fat, muscle, fluids, bones. i do not covet their white bodies
i do not worship tissues and organs other than my own

lucille, i am ten years old, and there is no first diet
i am wearing my pleated pep squad skirt
without storying the word "fat" onto each thigh
there are no catcalls of adult men through car windows
as i walk home from cheering at a fifth-grade baseball game

lucille, i am twelve years old, and there is no first abuser
i have learned to say the word *no*
i have learned to say the word *no*

above a whisper
i have learned to say the word *no*
    without an apology behind it

lucille, i am fourteen years old and reading
the diagnostic and statistical manual of mental disorders
i am confronting the diagnostic criteria for anorexia
and accepting the entry just how it reads
for the disorder that it is

as in
    i do not read the signs and symptoms
    as items to put on a to-do list

as in
    i do not revise the definition
    to replace it with one of my own creation:

        anorexia | an·o·rex·i·a | a-nə-ˈrek-sē-ə
        noun
        3. danielle, the truest indicator of your achievement of perfection

lucille, i am nineteen years old, and i understand starving
myself invisible is not the efficient, tactical approach
to avoid the stares or groping hands or thieving bodies
that don't ask for permission. i know that a calorie is energy,
and i need to be strong for battle

the strategy is clear: do not hide the prey
    turn the hunt on the predator

the strategy is clear: do not disappear the target
    devastate the marksmen

Note to Self

Dear ~~Wheezy~~ Danielle,

I don't know what compelled you to register for a half marathon or what exactly propelled you through that race. What I *do* know is that much of life feels like mile 11. You will start looking for exits.

What you will need from yourself then is to do *exactly* what you did during that race: Remember who you are. Trust your body to carry you until you cross the finish line. Do not stop moving. Just put one foot in front of the other.

We live in a world that is hostile toward compassion, one that prefers instead to send us messages that are akin to a coach who thinks the only way to motivate us is to tear us apart.

Do not berate yourself for having absorbed these lessons. Do not linger on the memories of using these learned words to tear yourself down.

You don't know this yet, but one day, you will be loved for your gentleness. You won't need to motivate yourself with criticism. That's never truly been your way, anyway.

Do use words to build yourself back up.

Do remember how incredibly powerful your words are.

How powerful *you* are.

* * *

...*at age 19*

CW: Details disordered eating behaviors and body image disturbance

Dear Danielle,

Don't remember kneeling on the floor. You've spent enough time down there. What I want you to remember is this:

You are the girl who picked herself up from the floor.

You drew water from the faucet you had, at first, turned on to drown out the sound. With this, a rinse of the mouth and a cleansing of the tears on your cheeks. Then you dried your face and went to the kitchen to honor your body and feed your hunger.

You are the girl who picked herself up from the floor.

You are not the starvation diets. You are not the aspirational magazine clippings.

You are the girl who picked herself up from the floor.

You are not the laxatives. You are not the dissected body that a past-you once reduced to parts—right thigh, abdomen, left thigh, collarbone. You are not the well-practiced purge.

You are the girl who picked herself up from the floor.

You are not a "before." You are not an entry in the *Diagnostic and Statistical Manual of Mental Disorders.*

You are the girl who picked herself up from the floor.

You took the skillful hands that you once used to erase yourself to instead push your body up from the tile and away from the porcelain of the toilet.

You are the girl who picked herself up from the floor.

The girl we needed you to be so that I can be the woman writing you this letter.

* * *

...*at age 9*

Dear Danielle,

You won't remember the word. Perhaps you blocked it out—the body's attempt to protect itself.

It's not the loss you will most remember, but what came after: Riding in the back of the minivan and locking eyes with a woman in a car who was crying too. You won't remember exactly what the woman looked like. Your vague memory will say to you that she was blond and in her late 20s or early 30s. Those details you will not place.

She did lift her hand to you, you know. Not exactly a wave, but a lift of the fingers.

The woman, the stranger—for the rest of your life, you will wonder who she is. You will wonder why she was crying. You will wonder what or who broke her. Is she still alive? Wonder if she's still broken. Does she remember the little girl in the back of the minivan? You will wish you raised your hand to meet hers. You will wonder what compelled her to wave to a stranger.

That's what you'll remember. How she noticed your tears, and you, instinctively, cocked your head to the left as you often did when trying to understand something.

And just for that moment, you were not a nine-year-old girl with a loss. You were just at the very beginning of learning that—if you look up—you are never truly alone.

Nearly 30 years later, I cannot stop thinking about and telling your story. I've shared it with friends, in classes, in workshops, and at story-telling events.

"I've tried to render this moment into a poem, but it just won't come. I don't know how to tell it," I said once, after sharing your story with a friend.

"Just like that," she said, "Tell it *exactly* like that."

Over the years, I've wondered why your story was so important to me. Other than the chance of two people stopped at the same intersection, crying at the same time, and locking eyes for just a moment, what was special about it?

The theory I've landed on is this:

Your shame felt so big that you didn't believe there was space for any other feeling in the universe.

And then there was.

A stranger thought you were worthy of notice when you didn't think you deserved it.

You don't have to *do* anything or *earn* attention and care. You just have value, and that's it.

A few final things I need you to know:

Mom wasn't disappointed in you. Mom was upset because she knew *you* would be upset. Mom knew you wanted to win, and she wanted you to have the desires of your heart. More than anything, I think, she was proud of her little girl. The shy little girl who was brave enough to join the school spelling bee even though you knew you'd have to stand on a stage to do so, because your love for words was stronger than your desire to hide.

In the school auditorium, you cried with your full body. You were loud and let emotion spill out of you. There was nothing small or restrained about the way you cried. You taught me that if my pain is big, cry big. Our emotions deserve a proportionate response.

If there is a moment when I am looking down, feeling defeated, I will remember to look up.

Have a story inside me, and I'm not sure how to tell it?

I will tell it however I need.

I will tell it *exactly* like that.

Claiming Space (Reprise)

In the backyard of a two-bedroom, one-bathroom pink house with white trim in South LA, a family of giants lived beneath the ground. Each time these imposing beings would emerge from the earth, they would announce their appearance with a signature rumble. As the ground shook, a crack would form in the concrete. The enormous beings would put one hand on each side of the crack, push their bodies up with all their strength, then crawl out of the earth and onto their feet, passing through the backyard toward the street. With each step, the ground gave a thunderous quake, and the landing of the giants' feet emitted a resounding *boom boom*.

The giants usually arrived when I was playing in the backyard. I would feel the tremors, then quickly run inside. Sometimes, I was too afraid to look. Other times, my fear lost to my curiosity, so I would peek through the bars on our door, as I couldn't tear my eyes away.

This was indeed very strange. *Giants? Where are they going? What do they want? And why do they live beneath the ground in my family's backyard?* Stranger still, I appeared to be the only one who noticed the giants or the tremors. I would look around me, and everyone in my family was calm. I would think, *Why is no one else terrified?! Everyone is going on with their day while the earth is opening beneath us!*

Perhaps these were dreams. How else would I explain it? Then again, I hesitate to call these giants the stuff of dreams, because not only did these encounters feel so real, with images so vivid, they happened more than once. I can still see the outline of their massive bodies if I think deeply enough. I still don't know exactly what this was.

* * *

I have brilliant friends. So brilliant, in fact, that I often take notes during our conversations. Years beyond, I find their words on sticky notes, loose scraps of paper, and receipts. Several years ago, I had brunch with a dear friend. The context of the conversation is lost to memory, but her words I scribbled on the café receipt are not: "Silence tells a lot of lies."

Your voice is unimportant. You don't deserve better. No one will believe you. They will dismiss or ridicule you. If you had controlled your body and protected it from predators, you would not have become prey. You don't belong here. You are a failure. You are worthless. Something must be wrong with you. It is your fault. No one will understand. If you told them, they would never look at you the same way. You are broken. You can't burden anyone with this. You're the only one who has ever felt this way.

Not only does silence tell a lot of lies, but my silence had not served me.

My lessons taught me to shrink, not to take up space with voice or body, not to object. To think of myself in terms of deficit, not strength. To view Blackness only in terms of its "unfortunate" distance from whiteness.

My lessons taught me to prepare myself for the next occurrence of an 8-year-old boy lifting my skirt on the playground in the name of a game I never agreed to join. To try to remain polite and likable even as a 14-year-old boy assaulted me. To temper my language in a sexual harassment report that I almost didn't file at all. To stay in a relationship with a man to protect his mental health to the detriment of my own.

My lessons prepared me for compliance, not liberation. For the silence that comes from waiting for directions on whom and how to be rather than the sound of my own feet landing as I stand up and assert my right to exist.

In silence, we believe the lie that we're the only ones inside the experience of something.

The lessons we internalize that hold us in silence are just as effective and insidious as the lessons that hold the promise of power, dominance, and control taught to those who benefit from our silence.

Founded in 2006 by activist and organizer Tarana Burke, the 'me too.' Movement was created to interrupt not only sexualized violence but the isolation that often accompanies it. Over a decade later, the #MeToo hashtag went viral on social media, with myriad posts and comments from people sharing their experiences of sexualized violence. What we witnessed with the 'me too.' Movement is a vibrant example of how one person breaking their silence gives another courage to do the same.

To the uninitiated, the deluge of such testimonies may seem jarring or appear to be a witch hunt, suggesting that accusations of sexualized violence is a new trend. What comes with speaking out against violence, though, is often more violence. Survivors are bombarded with accusations of lying, and—depending on their identities—the responses are often laden with hate speech. Any identity you have is means to insult and threaten you. Survivors receive death threats, and, yes, threats of sexual assault.

So, why speak? Why now?

You speak because you need to. You speak because you've been quiet long enough. You speak because someone else may need to hear you. You speak because speaking hurts less than silence. You speak because maybe someone will actually believe you this time. You speak because now there's enough distance—physical, temporal, psychological, or otherwise –between you and the person or event that silenced you.

* * *

In a graduate school seminar, I learned the term "confessional writing." Of the writers who wrote within the genre, two of the most prominent figures I learned are writers Anne Sexton and Sylvia Plath. These writers wrote about religion, familial relationships, sex, mental illness, death, female identity (especially the social norms that governed it), and all manner of subjects deemed personal. The work is often (but not always) autobiographical, writing the complexities of human lives in intimate detail—all without a veil.

Almost immediately after I learn the term "confessional writing," I learn many critics and readers truly detest confessional writing. Confessional narratives are often called narcissistic, self-indulgent, even navel-gazing. These pieces of writing make public what is traditionally private and—these critics and readers argue—should stay that way.

These topics belong in the realm of the bedroom, the family, the therapist's office, but certainly not in public. They should be spoken in a whisper, not a shout, if they are spoken at all. No one wants to read your journal. At least have the decency to suffer in silence like the rest of us.

That these writers shouted instead of whispered is *precisely* why I connect with this form.

In graduate school classes and at open mics, I always shared the "heavy" poems. I tried not to, but even when I set an intention to write a "happy" poem, I couldn't. Almost as though my body knew I was holding onto too much and refused to hold anything else.

She would not allow me to stay quiet.

Those emotions, thoughts, and experiences had been screaming to be let out, and they refused to be silent any longer. My stories were emerging from the place inside of me where I had contained them, and, with each impulse, I felt the foundation under which they were buried crack bit by bit. They erupted not with a whisper, but with a *boom*.

At open mics, I read and performed poems about sexualized violence, eating disorders, internalized oppression, and mental health crises. Others would read poems that they had written about nature, horses, and boats (this was the Pacific Northwest after all).

I would look around me, and everyone was calm.

Am I just really messed up? I would wonder.

Am I the only one experiencing the tremors?

* * *

In my TEDx Talk, I said, "I'm not up here for me; I'm doing this for that *one*, that silenced voice that doesn't seem to have a space."

Now, I do speak for me. But I also still speak to that silenced voice.

Those are my readers. My readers say to me, "We need more strong female voices like yours."

I don't show up for the critic with a roll in their eyes.

I show up for the reader with tears in theirs.

Not for the critic who thinks content warnings are side effects of a world gone too soft.

But for the survivor who has lived the content.

I have spent my entire life wanting to be accepted and palatable. I tried to be everyone's type and fit everyone's taste. I thought there was a way to be liked by every single human being on this planet. No one else had found the way yet, but I would. I would just need to try harder.

I would wait until I learned that secret and *then* I would speak.

I thought the price I would pay for speaking would be too steep, but the cost of staying quiet was far greater.

I once believed that silence is a passive act. It's not. It's a violent one. I had walked the world with my hands covering my own mouth.

The wisdom of my body revealed to me that I no longer had to fight. I could rest.

"Lay down your hands. You've been trying to control me for so long. Let me take over. Let me take care of you," she said.

Truly. Excellent. Comeback.

* * *

In the minutes before TEDxWWU began, I walked through the crowded lobby of the Performing Arts Center. The headset microphone was already taped to my cheek, and I felt somewhat on display. I looked at the faces—students, staff, faculty, and community members. A student asked if I was nervous. I responded that I was terrified, then continued, "I need to see the faces of the people in the audience. I need to remember why I'm doing this."

If they weren't just a mass of shapes in the dark theater, I would feel slightly less afraid. If I remembered that students I knew and cared about were in the audience, I would recall the importance of the words I was about to say. Regardless of the fear I felt or anything else, I *needed* to speak.

I could feel it in my bones.

When I looked out into the audience, there were indeed faces and bodies mostly hidden in darkness. What helped me remain on that stage for 19 minutes was that, when I looked out, I saw 150 anthologies —people living and collecting their own stories. Stories that perhaps they had never shared aloud.

To them, and to you, I want to say this:

May we know that we matter just as we are. No demolition necessary.

May we look anew at ourselves and say, "I *do* have value. I *am* art."

May we lay down our hands and uncover our mouths.

May we claim space for ourselves and for our stories.

May we give voice to all stories we had once contained in silence—
    however we need to unearth them. Be it a whisper or a shout.
    Standing before an audience or pen in hand with the journal page.

May we remind ourselves: Tell it however you need. Tell it *exactly* like that.

May we remember to look up.

May we know and feel that we are not alone.

May we never again look around us and wonder if we're the only ones experiencing the tremors.

Epilogue

Behold the last three sentences of my TEDxWWU audition video:

I even began to doubt myself on my fit to speak at TEDx, as if I had nothing important to share, because I maybe don't have the right credentials or experience. I think there's a narrow definition of who's qualified to speak as an authority, as a leader, and I want to challenge that. I can speak as someone who is still figuring this all out, someone who's still in that process of renovation.

I had forgotten that I said this. Because I had allowed TEDxWWU to become about something other than the message. The reason for the sleepless nights in the weeks before TEDx—and my reason for not watching my talk in the time since—can be narrowed down to one word: fear. Fear of what people would think about me. Fear that viewers would question my suitability as a speaker. Fear they would criticize me because of how I looked, how I dressed, and how I talked. Fear that I would make a mistake or become too overwhelmed by emotion to speak, and my embarrassment would be public, living in perpetuity on the internet and in the minds of all present.

I can speak as someone who is still figuring this all out, someone who's still in that process of renovation. And yet, I allowed myself to feel as though I failed because I didn't deliver the talk perfectly.

But to speak as a person who is in the process of revision? If that was my goal?

Well, then...perfect.

Resources

EATING DISORDERS

National Association of Anorexia Nervosa and Associated Disorders
Website: anad.org
Helpline: 888-375-7767

National Eating Disorders Association
Website: nationaleatingdisorders.org
Helpline: 1-800-931-2237 (Toll-Free)
24/7 crisis support: Text "NEDA" to 741741

INTIMATE PARTNER/DOMESTIC VIOLENCE

National Coalition Against Domestic Violence
Through collective action, the NCADV engages in efforts to identify and address the systemic factors that contribute to domestic violence. This survivor-led organization provides programs to support survivors, increase public awareness, build capacity of advocates, and promote public policy to eliminate domestic violence. ncadv.org

National Domestic Violence Hotline
Website: thehotline.org
Hotline: 800-799-SAFE (7233)
Receive 24/7 support via text message: Text "START" to 88788

MENTAL HEALTH

National Alliance on Mental Illness (NAMI)
Helpline: 1-800-950-NAMI (6264) or info@nami.org
Receive 24/7 crisis support via text message: text "NAMI" to 741741

National Suicide Prevention Lifeline
suicidepreventionlifeline.org
800-273-TALK (8255)
Trained crisis counselors are available 24/7

To Write Love on Her Arms: A non-profit organization committed to reducing barriers to mental health care for people struggling with addiction, depression, self-injury, and suicidal ideation. TWLOHA connects people with resources and offers a scholarship program to reduce financial barriers to treatment and recovery. twloha.com

SEXUALIZED VIOLENCE

me too. International: me too. International is committed to changing the conversation about sexual violence to center the needs, experiences, and healing of survivors who are often ignored or discounted in mainstream narratives about sexual violence. metoomvmt.org

National Sexual Violence Resource Center: An organization dedicated to preventing and responding to sexual violence. NSVRC also maintains a directory to help connect survivors of sexual violence with local organizations that provide support services. nsvrc.org

Rape, Abuse & Incest National Network (RAINN)
Website: rainn.org
National Sexual Assault Hotline: 800-656-HOPE (4673)
Receive support via online chat: online.rainn.org

Permissions

I extend my gratitude to the following for permission to reprint previously published material:

Excerpt from "my dream about being white" from *How to Carry Water: Selected Poems of Lucille Clifton*. Copyright © 1987 by Lucille Clifton. Reprinted with the permission of The Permissions Company, LLC on behalf of BOA Editions Ltd., boaeditions.org.

Excerpt from "Diego, Frida, & Me" by Molly Crabapple, *The Paris Review*, March 2013. Used by permission of author and publisher.

"Song for My Beloved I: Loving" was originally published in *As/Us: A Space for Women of the World*, Issue 3.

I do not reproduce any material from the following, but I briefly share my experience with the practice and workbook:

Neff, K. & Germer, C. (2018) *The Mindful Self-Compassion Workbook*. New York: Guilford Press. Permission granted by the Center for Mindful Self-Compassion, centerformsc.org.

Credits

Cover design by Federica Dias
Author photo by Jon Smith Photography

With Gratitude

My family: Mom and Dad—my first teachers—you know how sometimes there's that one teacher who you clashed with, but then you got older and respected the heck out of them? That's you (and Ms. Cagle). To my big brother and sisters, thanks for letting me tag along since 1984.

The Ladies: Cheers and pinkies up! to four of the funniest, smartest, and most resilient women I've ever known. I love us.

My friends: Thank you for being the kind of people that inspire me so much I take notes when we talk. p.s. Laurel: Your turn.

Elena ("Dr. P"): I miss singing and dancing to Motown hits with you. Thanks for modeling a life well lived.

My therapists: I didn't/don't always do the homework but thank you for the lessons and emotion wheel handouts.

My students: You taught me so much about resilience and being human.

Alex Franzen, Lindsey Smith, and the Tiny Book Course team: Thanks for the inspiration, dog photos, and encouragement to make imperfect art.

Ms. Lawson: My middle school language arts teacher who foresaw a book in my future. Took almost three decades, but I did it!

George: Not sure how the afterlife works, so you may not see these words, but you changed my world. I'm glad you were in my classroom, too.

About Danielle Shontae Smith

Photo: © Jon Smith Photography

Danielle Shontae Smith is a writer, storyteller, and educator. Smith writes poetry and nonfiction about a range of topics, from the intersectionality of ethnic and gender identity to mental health and body image. Smith earned an MA in English–Creative Writing from Western Washington University and a BA in Women's Studies from UCLA, with emphases in social inequality and literature. In both her professional and creative work, Smith has explored how individuals and communities use the medium of language for personal development, connection, and in movements for social change. She believes in the transformative power of story and has performed at and hosted live storytelling events. Smith lives in Southern California and tries to visit the ocean weekly to make peace with the high cost of living.

To learn more, visit her website: msdaniellesmith.com.

www.ingramcontent.com/pod-product-compliance
Lightning Source LLC
Chambersburg PA
CBHW020237130626
46549CB00005B/1935